Beginner's Guide to
POTTERY & CERAMICS

Everything you need to know to start making beautiful ceramics

Jacqui Atkin

Search Press

A QUARTO BOOK

Published in 2017 by
Search Press Ltd
Wellwood
North Farm Road
Kent TN2 3DR

ISBN: 978-1-78221-559-2

Conceived, designed and produced by
Quarto Publishing plc
The Old Brewery
6 Blundell Street
London N7 9BH
www.quartoknows.com

QUAR.PBA

Project editor: Liz Pasfield
Art editor: Claire van Rhyn
Assistant art director: Penny Cobb
Copy editor: Sally MacEachern
Designer: Tanya Devonshire-Jones
Photographer: Ian Howes
Picture research: Claudia Tate

Art director: Moira Clinch
Publisher: Samantha Warrington

Manufactured by
Printed in China by Hung Hing

10 9 8 7 6 5 4 3 2 1

FSC
www.fsc.org
MIX
Paper from
responsible sources
FSC® C017606

PUBLISHER'S NOTE
Working with pottery can be hazardous.
Always follow the instructions carefully, and
exercise caution. Follow the safety
procedures mentioned. As far as the
techniques and methods described in this
book are concerned, all statements,
information, and advice given are believed
to be accurate. However, neither the author,
the copyright holder, nor the publisher can
accept any legal liability.

CONTENTS

INTRODUCTION

Clay is an amazingly exciting material that has been used to make practical and decorative items since prehistoric times. The history of clay parallels the history of human civilization and its changing needs.

Some of the earliest clay shapes were votive objects used in ritual worship. Once formed into a shape, the clay was likely hardened by baking it in the sun. The development of agriculture around 10,000–8,000 BCE created a need for vessels to store and contain food. Exactly when humans discovered that fire would make clay more durable will never be known, but it was probably accidental. However, the discovery encouraged the development of a more deliberate approach to the manipulation of clay.

The fired surface of clay is a wonderful canvas for trying out creative designs.

Pottery became an important skill that was handed down through generations. Original clay bodies were coarse and fired in the open at low temperatures, but even the earliest examples show aesthetic consideration in the form of rudimentary impressed detail or slip decoration. Pots were often burnished, a technique that enabled them to hold fluid. Such examples, dating back to 6,000 BCE, have been found in Azerbaijan and other parts of Europe.

DEVELOPMENT OF TECHNIQUES

The versatility of clay must have changed the way people were able to live, but they quickly would have become aware of its limitations also. Clay can crack at both the forming and firing stages; forms can easily sag if the clay is too wet, or collapse when its weight is too great to hold a shape. Forming techniques undoubtedly were developed to cope with these limitations. Indeed, hand-building techniques have changed very little over the centuries. Some cultures still make pottery in exactly the same way as their ancestors, using rudimentary tools and firing outdoors in pits and basic kilns. The integrity and spontaneity of such ethnic potters have been a great source of inspiration to many Western potters, particularly from the mid-20th century onwards.

The discovery that certain types of clay could be fired at higher temperatures, thus vitrifying the body and making the wares much more durable, was made in ancient China and Japan. It was there,

The development of firing techniques and glazes was an important stage in the history of pottery.

too, that glaze was developed to colour and texture the surface of the clay. Although form was paramount, every stage of the ceramic process was thoroughly considered. Excessive surface decoration was deemed unnecessary – much more important was the effect of the fire on raw clay.

The joy of working with clay is in creating decorative and functional objects.

USING THIS BOOK

Today, clay is still a unique material that offers endless opportunity for personal expression, whether the maker wants to create decorative, sculptural or functional work. This book aims to provide the beginner with all the basic technical information needed to get started.

Getting Started begins with information about tools, basic equipment and clays – their types, properties, preparation and handling. There are also basic skills that teach you how to prepare clay for all the different forming processes, and decorative surface treatments.

Techniques and Projects demonstrates the construction processes. Each technique is followed by a project that puts all the relevant skills into practice, from making and decorating to firing. Step-by-step photographs and clear instructions guide you through the processes. Cross-references direct you to relevant techniques in the Basic Skills and Decorating sections.

The Surface Decoration Library contains examples of all the surface treatments demonstrated on pages 34–47 to provide alternative options for decorating the projects.

Techniques are easy to learn and the beginner will quickly pick up new skills.

This book is designed to give you an understanding of the skills required to work with clay and build up your confidence. It is by no means a definitive guide – most potters develop their own individual approach to clay once they have mastered the basic skills. It is important to understand that the book is not an end in itself, but a starting point from which to develop your own methods, ideas and unique style.

J. P. Allcin.

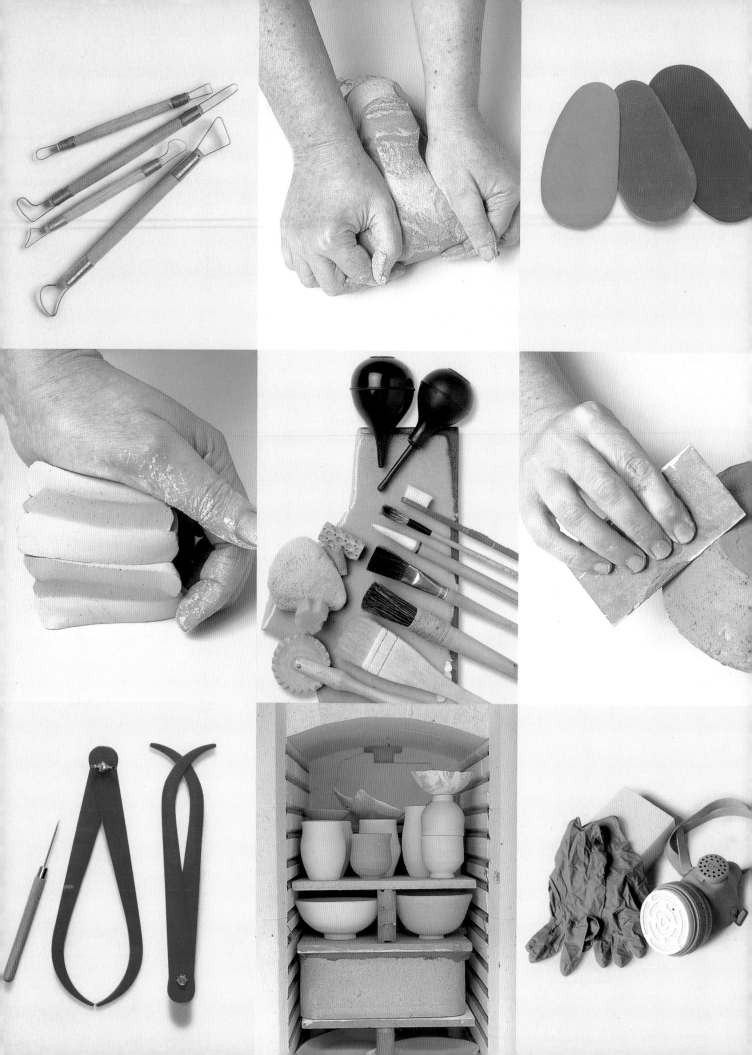

GETTING STARTED

Pottery is a very exciting journey of discovery, with plenty of scope for self-expression, but in order to start you need to know what tools and equipment are required. In addition, you need to learn the basic techniques. This section introduces you to the tools and equipment and suggests home-made alternatives. It discusses health and safety, and outlines the principles of good working practices. After an introduction to clay and pottery bodies, there is a very important section on clay preparation. Finally, you move on to basic skills and decorating to learn the first forming techniques and how to decorate the surface of your pots. It will really help your understanding of the subject if you read through this section before you begin working, so that you can develop your talent in an informed way.

The most important thing to remember about pottery is that nothing need ever be wasted. If your attempts are unsuccessful the first time, you can easily reclaim the clay and begin again. Everything takes a little practice, so be patient and, more importantly, have fun.

BASIC TOOLS

Pottery requires very few tools and many can be made or adapted from kitchen utensils and other household items. There are, however, a few essentials, which can be bought from pottery suppliers.

SCRAPING AND CUTTING TOOLS

POTTER'S NEEDLE Useful for marking levels on rims while the work is rotating on a banding wheel prior to cutting, and for piercing holes or releasing air. A good alternative is a large needle fixed into the end of a bottle cork.

CUTTING WIRE Essential for wedging clay and cutting pots off a wheel head, wires are usually about 46 cm (18 in.) long with wooden toggles at each end. You can make one to any length from fishing wire of a suitable thickness and coat-toggle buttons.

HOLE CUTTER Available in a variety of sizes, usually with a tapering metal blade. The cutter is rotated as it is pushed through the clay to make holes of different sizes.

METAL KIDNEY Used to refine the clay surface, it is generally available in several different sizes, grades and shapes – from oval to square – as well as with a serrated edge for paring down rough surfaces.

POTTER'S KNIFE Potter's knives make the cutting of wet clay easier. A hacksaw blade, sharpened at one end, works equally well, and the serrated edge makes a handy extra tool. Craft knives are also useful.

RIBBON OR LOOP TOOLS Used to trim the bases of wheel-thrown pots, but also to hollow out handmade shapes, especially sculptural forms.

RUBBER KIDNEY Used for the very fine smoothing and compacting of clay surfaces.

RASP (SURFORM) BLADE Used to pare down clay surfaces, level rims and create decorative surface texture. The blades are available in different sizes.

PAINT SCRAPER Useful for cleaning work surfaces and boards, especially dry plaster splashes from mouldmaking.

FORMING TOOLS

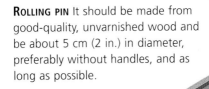

ROLLING PIN It should be made from good-quality, unvarnished wood and be about 5 cm (2 in.) in diameter, preferably without handles, and as long as possible.

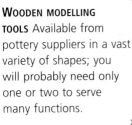

BANDING WHEEL OR TURNTABLE Not strictly essential, it makes most tasks easier because the work can be rotated and viewed from all sides.

ROLLER GUIDES Roller guides of varying thickness are indispensable for slab building; you will need two of each.

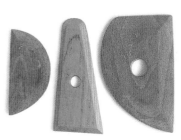

WOODEN MODELLING TOOLS Available from pottery suppliers in a vast variety of shapes; you will probably need only one or two to serve many functions.

WOODEN RIBS Mostly used for smoothing and refining wheel-thrown pots, but available in shapes to suit any kind of work.

CALLIPERS Used for measuring the widths of lids and galleries in the throwing process.

WOODEN SPOONS AND SPATULAS Easily sourced from your kitchen, these tools are highly versatile for beating, smoothing and texturing clay. Do not reuse in the kitchen.

DECORATING TOOLS

BRUSHES Good brushes are essential and should include soft, moplike varieties such as the hake for applying slips and glazes and small paintbrushes for underglazes and lustre details. Toothbrushes are useful for scoring and slipping joints in the clay and for spattering slip decoration. Shaving brushes are useful for brushing away bits of clay when carving or incising.

SPONGES All potters need a selection of natural and synthetic sponges to remove excess water from the insides and surfaces of pots, to smooth rims and to apply slip and glaze decoration. A sponge on a stick is useful for removing water from the inside of tall or narrow forms when throwing on the wheel.

SLIP TRAILERS These have a range of uses and are available in different sizes.

HOME-MADE TOOLS FOR SHAPING, TEXTURING AND STAMPING Very useful tools can be made from old credit cards, which can be cut to shape to suit the purpose. Old mascara wands are great for neatening holes. Many kitchen gadgets, like onion holders, can be used for texturing the surface of clay. Stamps for texturing can be made in clay and bisque fired, but objects such as buttons or old pieces of jewellery also work well.

POTTERY WHEEL

This is an incredibly expensive item for the beginner so you should try to master all the hand-building techniques first to assess your interest and dedication. Wheels are available in a variety of sizes and you should choose the one you feel most comfortable using. Look for secondhand models in good condition.

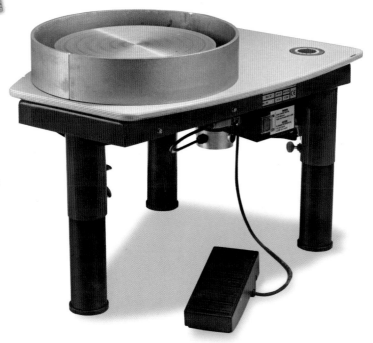

HEALTH AND SAFETY

WHEN WORKING WITH CLAY AND OTHER RELATED MATERIALS:

1. Never eat, drink or smoke in the workshop.

2. Always work in a suitably ventilated room with easy-to-clean, impermeable work surfaces, and facilities for washing close by.

3. Avoid generating airborne dust. It is better to prevent dust than to try to control it. To minimize hazards:

- Clean up spills immediately. This applies to liquids as well as powders because all materials become dust when they have dried. Spills on the floor also pose the risk of slipping.
- Clean all tools and equipment at the end of the working day.
- Use a vacuum cleaner with a filter for fine dust, not a brush, to clean all surfaces. After vacuuming, wash all surfaces.

4. Wear gloves when handling any colouring agents or oxides.

5. Wear a respirator (face mask) when handling powders.

6. Wear protective clothing. Try not to wipe dirty hands on your apron, as this will create dust when dry. Wash work clothing regularly.

7. Store dry materials in airtight, plastic containers to prevent bags breaking open and spilling dust into the atmosphere.

8. When sanding or fettling (turning or cleaning) dry or bisque-fired pots, wear a respirator and goggles to protect your nose and eyes.

9. Check that your tetanus immunization is up to date. Remember that clay is essentially dug from the ground and may carry bacteria that can cause infection in open wounds.

10. Keep a first-aid kit in the workshop. Protect cuts and scratches from contact with any ceramic materials.

 ## DANGEROUS MATERIALS

Some materials used in pottery as colourants for clays and glazes can be harmful if breathed in or ingested. Some studies suggest that certain materials can even be absorbed through the skin. Be sure to wear the appropriate protection when handling the following materials:

HIGHLY TOXIC
Lead, cadmium, antimony and barium.

USE WITH CARE
All colourants, especially copper oxide and carbonate, cobalt oxide and carbonate, chromium oxide, lithium oxide, zinc, strontium, nickel oxide and slip and glaze stains.

Borax, boron, boric acid, silica, quartz, flint, feldspar, China clay, ball clay, whiting and dolomite.

Pottery suppliers should always provide the relevant health and safety data for their products, and information relating to each material should be printed on the container. Be sure to read it!

CLAY

In its natural state, clay can be found almost anywhere in the world. Clay in its raw state is not very pliable, making it difficult to work with and requiring the addition of other materials to make it pliable.

The basic components of clay are silica and alumina. Natural clay is formed over millions of years from feldspathic or granite rocks, which have been decomposed through the action of weather and glaciers. Clays that are still where they were originally formed are known as residual or primary clays, and are fairly rare. The most important primary clay is kaolin (China clay). It is very pure and white with a large particle size that makes it very short (nonplastic), and thus unsuitable for use on its own. Bentonite is an extremely fine, plastic primary clay, which is added to shorter clays to increase their plasticity.

Clays that have been further eroded and weathered are known as secondary or sedimentary clays. They have been moved from their original source by water, wind or glacier. Such clays have fine particles and are very plastic. Ball clays are included in this group. In the process of travelling, the clays pick up minerals and impurities, making them suitable only for low-firing temperatures.

CLAY TYPES

Before choosing a clay for your project, you should consider what you want to make, how it will be fired and the final result you hope to achieve. Ask your supplier to recommend a suitable clay.

Here is a selection of commercial clays in their raw state and in their three main groups. The colour can change dramatically after firing, but your supplier should be able to show you fired samples before you buy.

EARTHENWARE

The most common and the least expensive clay, earthenware has a high iron content, giving it a rich, rusty colour. Earthenware has a firing temperature of 1000–1180°C (1832–2156°F). It does not vitrify (become glasslike), and so needs to be glazed if it will contain liquids. The glaze must be craze-resistant, to prevent liquids and foods from being absorbed into the clay body, and lead-free to prevent poisoning.

White earthenware makes an ideal choice for decoration with coloured slips or stains. It has a firing range of 1060–1180°C (1940–2156°F).

Earthenware of both types is a good choice for throwing on the wheel, but less so for hand building because it has a low resistance to warping.

RED EARTHENWARE
Fires to a rich terracotta – suitable for throwing and some hand building – particularly suited to various forms of slip decoration – used to make some domestic wares.

WHITE EARTHENWARE
Grey before firing and creamy white after – used in the same way as the red variety, but gives a brighter colour response for decoration.

SMOOTH BUFF CLAY
Fires to a creamy pink – wide firing range makes it suitable for earthenware and stoneware finishes.

STONEWARE

Stoneware clays are much stronger than earthenware; their density and hardness when fired give them their name. They can be fired to very high temperatures of 1200–1300°C (2192–2372°F), which cause the clay particles to fuse (vitrify), making the pot impervious to fluids. Items only need to be glazed for hygienic, decorative or aesthetic purposes.

There is a wide selection of stoneware clays available, in colours ranging from white to dark brown and compositions ranging from very smooth to very coarse. Most bodies are prepared from a mixture of plastic clays and minerals; some are multifunctional and can be used to throw on the wheel and hand build.

WHITE STONEWARE
Fires to white – medium textured, containing several grades of molochite (calcined China clay) – suited to throwing, coiling, hand building, modelling and fine sculpture.

SANDSTONE STONEWARE
Blend of low-iron-bearing clays – fires buff to light grey – ideal background for a more decorative approach.

GROGGED STONEWARE
Heavily grogged – textured but highly plastic – firing to a speckled grey-buff colour – suited to slab work – good choice for Raku or smoke firing.

SPECIAL STONEWARE
Blend of low shrinkage clays and calcined China clay – medium texture, excellent plasticity, low shrinkage and a wide firing range – great choice for smoke firing, Raku or stoneware decoration – fires to an ivory or off-white colour.

PORCELAIN

Porcelain is the whitest firing of all the clay bodies and the purest. It can be fired up to 1300°C (2372°F); at this temperature it is very hard and nonporous and can be incredibly translucent if worked thinly.

Porcelain is the most difficult clay to handle and is not the best material for the beginner. In addition, porcelain can distort significantly in the firing.

Practice and a delicate touch will enable you to master this clay. Only one project in this book is made from porcelain (see pages 106–107). Try it to see if you have the patience to work with it; or you can use white stoneware or earthenware instead.

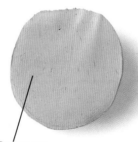

PORCELAIN
The ultimate white-firing stoneware clay – generally very fine textured – suitable for throwing, fine slabbing, modelling and casting in moulds.

CLAY STORAGE
Keep your clay stored in tightly sealed plastic bags to retain moisture, preferably in a dark, cool, frost-free place. Unfortunately, even in these conditions, the clay will eventually dry out, so check it from time to time. If it seems to be getting too hard, try wrapping it in an old, wet towel and sealing it back in a plastic bag for a few days. If too hard to handle, allow it to dry out completely and then reclaim it (see page 16).

CLAY CONSISTENCY

The consistency of clay directly relates to the item being made and the technique to be used. For example, hard slabbing calls for firm clay, coiling for more malleable clay and throwing clay needs to be relatively soft. Generally speaking, all clays should be soft enough to mould in the fingers without being sticky. If the clay is too soft it can be firmed up by kneading it on a plaster bat, or other porous surface, to remove excess water. Hard clay can often be saved by wedging in softer clay. If it is too hard, it should be dried out and reclaimed (see page 16).

READY-MADE CLAYS

Clay shrinks as it dries and then more as it is fired. You can generally expect your clay to shrink between 10–15 per cent, depending on its type and the firing temperature. Clay can warp as it dries, but the problem can usually be alleviated by the addition of sand or grog.

Pottery suppliers stock a range of clays and should be able to provide information about shrinkage rates, suitability for a particular making method and firing temperatures, as well as helpful advice to resolve any problems. Ask your supplier for samples to test for suitability.

RECLAIMING CLAY

One of the best things about working with clay is that there is very little waste. Until it is fired it can be reprocessed again and again without detriment. Reclaim each type of clay in separate buckets, or save them together to make a mixed body. Always test the mixed clay body before making a piece of work.

SHRINKAGE

To measure your clay for shrinkage, roll out some sample slabs and cut them into 15-cm (6-in.) long strips. Draw a 10-cm (4-in.) long line down the centre of the strips. Measure the line when the clay has dried, after it has been bisque fired, and after it has been fired to its top temperature.

If you are testing several clays, it will help to number the samples because fired clays can look very similar. Make a note of your results for future reference.

1 Allow the clay to dry out completely. Break it into small pieces and place it in a large plastic container. Completely cover the clay with warm water and allow it to break down overnight – this process is called slaking down.

2 Siphon off the excess water with a slip trailer. Give the clay slurry a little mix and transfer it to a plaster bat to form a layer about 5 cm (2 in.) thick.

3 Check the clay from time to time. When it has dried to a stage where it can be lifted easily from the bat, turn the clay over so that the wetter slurry on the surface comes into contact with the plaster. When the clay has firmed up to a workable consistency, remove it from the bat and wedge it (see below).

CLAY PREPARATION

As with many other crafts, preparation is vital for a successful outcome.

WEDGING

Wedging mixes the clay thoroughly and removes air bubbles that could cause the clay to shatter when fired. The technique shown can be used to blend two or more clay types together or to combine hard and soft layers of a particular clay.

1 **LAYERING THE CLAY** Slice the two blocks of clay into sheets with a cutting wire. Stack them in alternate layers. Beat the pile into a brick with your hand.

2 Position the cutting wire under the raised end, as close to the centre as possible. Cut the block in half.

3 Lift one half then throw it forcibly on top of the other half. Beat the clay back to a brick shape. Repeat until the two clays are completely combined.

KNEADING

Kneading is essential to even out the clay body and remove air bubbles, which can cause bloating or explosions during firing. Badly prepared clay will lead to very disappointing results.

Water constantly evaporates from clay. Kneading redistributes the water. Prepare only enough clay to complete the project and keep it sealed in plastic until needed.

SPIRAL KNEADING

This technique is more difficult to master than ox-head kneading, but it is useful for larger amounts of clay.

1 Place your hands on opposite sides of a roughly rounded mass of clay. With your right hand, push down on the clay while rolling it forwards. Contain the clay with your left hand to prevent sideways movement. Use your left hand to rotate the clay mass after each forwards movement.

2 A cut through the clay mass from time to time will show a developing spiral as the clays mix. Continue to rotate the clay anticlockwise, moving the right hand into position for each downwards push. Try to develop a rhythm as you work.

OX-HEAD KNEADING

Many potters find this the easier of the two methods demonstrated.

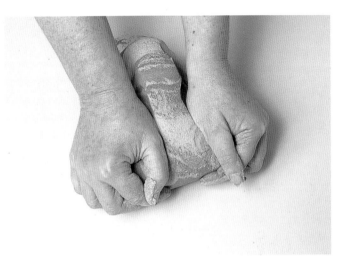

1 Position the hands on opposite sides of the clay mass with the heels over the top and the fingers wrapped around the sides. Push the clay down and away from the body, digging the palms into the clay so that a raised mass remains in the centre. Roll the clay back towards the body and reposition the hands slightly forwards. Repeat the rolling and pushing.

2 Continue to knead the clay by rocking and pushing until it is smooth and thoroughly mixed with no air pockets.

KILNS AND FIRING

Without doubt, the kiln is the most expensive item you are ever likely to need. Do not rush into a decision but look at all the available models offered by as many suppliers as possible. There can be quite substantial differences in price between suppliers for similar models.

Beginners are generally best advised to fire in an electric kiln because the outcome of the firing is the most predictable. All the projects in this book were fired in an electric kiln; some had their second firing in a Raku kiln (see page 20).

Electric kilns are generally the most suitable for urban environments because they fire cleanly, whereas gas or wood kilns create fumes and smoke. Electric kilns are available in a vast range of sizes, the smallest of which can be fired in a domestic situation. Sophisticated firing controllers will program every stage of the firing and mean that you do not have to be with the kiln while it fires.

Top-loading electric kilns

TOP-LOADING ELECTRIC KILNS
Top-loading kilns are ideal for the beginner because they tend to be cheaper to buy, will fit into small-scale workshops and are easier to install.

POINTS TO CONSIDER
- Accessibility to your premises. The kiln must fit through the door.
- The scale of your work and the quantity you produce. If you need to fire something in a hurry and your kiln is big, you will waste energy.
- Safety aspects. A kiln should not be in the room where you work. If it has to be, you should not be in the room while it is firing. Firing overnight can be the solution. A kiln should be located so you have enough space to move around it and away from flammable materials or structures.
- Power supply to your workshop. Some small kilns can be plugged into your normal household supply, but the bigger the kiln, the greater the power supply required.
- The strength of the floor in your workshop.

A front-loading kiln

FRONT-LOADING KILNS
Generally, front-loading kilns have a more solid metal framework and the firebrick wall is more substantial, which means it retains heat for much longer. This type of kiln is much harder wearing than the top-loading version but is more expensive to buy and install. It is also much heavier.

NEW VERSUS OLD
If you can afford it, you are best advised to buy a new kiln because older kilns tend to be heavier and more expensive to fire. They can also be a false economy because they may need expensive overhauling. However, great bargains can be had from people who have bought new kilns but then lost interest in pottery.

FIRING YOUR KILN

All objects made in clay have to be fired to make them permanent and functional. During firing, the real alchemy of pottery happens as the raw clay goes through a chemical change and becomes ceramic.

Beginners often find the prospect of firing their work daunting, but it is not a mystery and your confidence will build with experience. It will help if you record the results of your firing. Note all the details of your work, like glaze combinations, thickness of application or decorative techniques. You can easily forget what you did on a pot to make it fabulous – if you did not make a note, it can never be repeated.

Pottery generally has two firings: the first bisque, or biscuit, firing hardens the clay in preparation for secondary treatments like glaze; the second glaze firing is usually at a higher temperature and adds a protective and decorative coat. The glaze firing may be to earthenware or stoneware temperatures.

KILN SUPPORTS AND PACKING

Kilns are packed using shelves and supports. Tubular supports are available in different sizes and heights and are stackable. To raise glazed work off the kiln shelf, triangular "star stilts" are used. The points break off after firing, but can leave a tiny mark, which will need to be ground down.

A variety of tubular supports and "star stilts".

PACKING A KILN FOR BISQUE FIRING

It does not matter if the pots touch one another. Bowls can be stacked rim to rim, or base to base, as long as the weight is evenly distributed. Some pots can be fired inside others for economy, but they must fit freely and loosely. If they are wedged, they will crack when the clay shrinks.

A packed kiln ready for bisque firing

PACKING A KILN FOR GLAZE FIRING

It is essential that the pots do not touch one another. The kiln shelf must be coated with kiln wash to prevent glaze drips sealing the pot onto the shelf. This is especially important for high-temperature firings. Kiln wash can be bought from your supplier or made from a mix of two parts alumina and one part China clay.

KILN FIRING TIMES AND TEMPERATURES

This kiln chart shows the approximate cycles recommended for successful firing of your pottery.

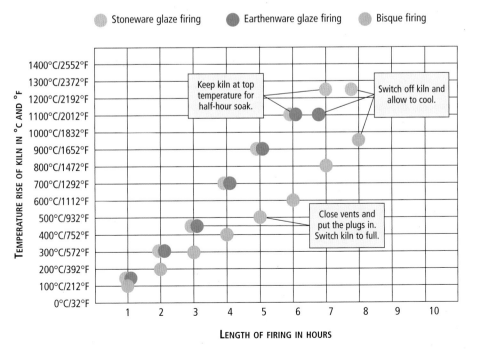

● Stoneware glaze firing   ● Earthenware glaze firing   ● Bisque firing

Keep kiln at top temperature for half-hour soak.

Switch off kiln and allow to cool.

Close vents and put the plugs in. Switch kiln to full.

TEMPERATURE RISE OF KILN IN °C AND °F

1400°C/2552°F
1300°C/2372°F
1200°C/2192°F
1100°C/2012°F
1000°C/1832°F
900°C/1652°F
800°C/1472°F
700°C/1292°F
600°C/1112°F
500°C/932°F
400°C/752°F
300°C/572°F
200°C/392°F
100°C/212°F
0°C/32°F

LENGTH OF FIRING IN HOURS

SMOKE FIRING

This is an ancient form of firing that is still very popular for its special effects. It is a low-firing technique and the pottery should not be bisque fired above 1000°C (1832°F), otherwise it will not be porous enough to absorb the carbon from the fire.

Smoking is usually combined with burnishing and often with clay resist slips, which allow the surface to be patterned in various ways. The results can be incredibly dramatic, but work fired directly in the smoke without surface treatments is equally exciting.

The simplest and most inexpensive kiln for smoke firing is a metal container, such as a dustbin, with a few holes drilled at intervals around the side to allow for the passage of air. The source of smoke is usually sawdust, straw or newspaper.

1 **PACKING THE KILN** For pots covered in a resist slip the quickest and easiest method of firing is in newspaper. Place the pot in a bin filled with loosely scrunched newspaper and set it alight. The process may have to be repeated for good effect. Alternatively, you can fire in sawdust, which simply involves packing the pot so that it is covered and allowing it to burn down slowly, covered with a lid.

2 **CLEANING OFF THE RESIST** When the pot has been fired two or three times, remove the slurry resist with a metal kidney. If the pot is still hot, use a heavy-duty glove to hold it.

3 Polish with beeswax to restore the shine.

RAKU FIRING

The term "Raku" comes from the Japanese for happiness or enjoyment. It is an incredibly exciting and spectacular method of firing, but the pieces are more decorative than functional. Two of the projects have been Raku fired (see pages 68 and 90).

RAKU KILNS
Raku kilns can be built from firebricks or high-temperature insulating bricks. For more rapid firings, the kiln can be made from metal drums or wire-mesh cages and lined with ceramic fibre for insulation. Commercial gas burners are widely available and make firing quick, clean and easy. Ask your supplier for details.

FIRING PROCEDURE
Normally, open, grogged clays with good thermal-shock properties are used for Raku. The pots are given a normal bisque firing to 1000°C (1832°F) before being glazed and placed in the Raku kiln, which is most often fired using propane gas. The firing usually takes place outside because of the fumes. The pots are rapidly fired until the glaze melts. Raku glazes melt between 800–1000°C (1472–1832°F), and firing usually takes 20–30 minutes. The pots are lifted, still red-hot and glowing, from the kiln with tongs, and placed in drums of wood shavings. Because of the rapid cooling process, the pots undergo intense thermal shock, which causes the glaze to craze, allowing smoke to penetrate through to the clay body. This gives the familiar crackle effect.

SAFETY
Raku firing involves working with pots at extreme temperatures and can be hazardous. To reduce the risk, you should have adequate gloves, protective clothing, masks, goggles and tongs to lift the pots from the kiln. Keep a bucket of water, or a fire extinguisher, close by in case of accidents.

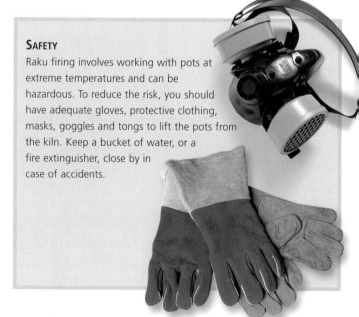

1 **FIRING** Fire the pot on a triangular "star stilt" to raise it off the kiln floor until the glaze melts and the pot glows. Remove the kiln lid and put it safely to one side. Wearing heavy-duty gloves and a respirator, lift the pot from the kiln with metal tongs. You do not have to rush.

2 **THE REDUCTION BIN** Transfer the glowing pot to the bin of wood shavings. It will ignite quickly, so do not stay too close. Cover the pot with a little more of the shavings. Seal the lid down firmly.

3 **REMOVING THE GLAZE** If the pot was coated in a resist slip and glaze, both can be removed with a metal kidney and then a soft cloth when the pot is cool enough to handle.

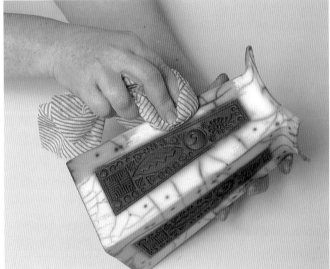

4 **CLEANING A GLAZED SURFACE** Permanent glazes can be cleaned with a scouring pad. They will generally look black when lifted out of the reduction bin, but can be transformed to reveal a lustrous surface.

TIPS FOR SUCCESS

- Have absolutely everything you need ready before starting the firing.
- Make sure that the reduction bin is easy to access when you lift the work from the kiln.
- Position the kiln on a good flat surface.
- Have someone with you when you fire; it is safer and much more fun to share the experience.

Basic Skills

When you start to work with clay, there are some basic skills that you will need to learn in order to progress. Although there are no real hard and fast rules in pottery, and most potters develop their own methods of doing things as they begin to understand the clay and the processes, we all need a starting point and some guidelines for development. In this section you will learn all the basic skills required to make a start. The projects will help you develop these skills as you create different shapes and surfaces. Hopefully, they will also inspire you to develop ideas of your own. Have fun practising. Clay is never wasted because it can always be reclaimed!

Pinching to make a simple bowl

Pinching is a simple technique and produces immediate results. Aim for a wall thickness of 13 mm (½ in.). With practice you will be able to pinch the walls thinner, but start with a thicker wall of clay that you can later pinch out a little thinner.

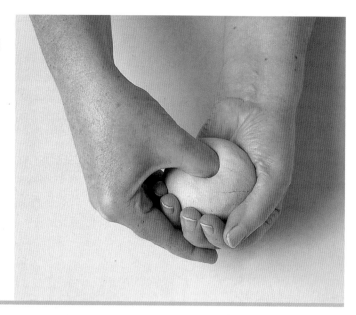

1 A small amount of clay will pinch out a long way, so form some well-prepared clay into a smooth ball that will fit comfortably in the palm of one hand. Using the thumb of the other hand, press down through the centre of the clay until you feel some pressure in the palm of the hand holding the ball. Measure the thickness at the base between the thumb and forefinger.

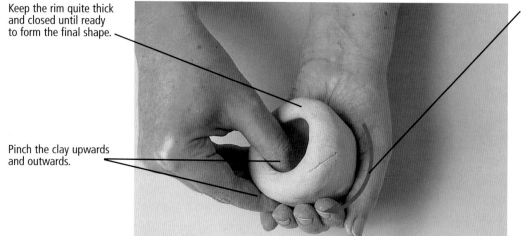

Keep the rim quite thick and closed until ready to form the final shape.

Rotate the clay clockwise as you pinch.

Pinch the clay upwards and outwards.

2 Use your finger and thumb to begin pinching out the shape from the bottom of the ball. Work in small, close movements, rotating the clay in the palm of your hand in a rhythmic action to even out the marks made by your fingers.

TIPS TO CONTROL THE SHAPE
- Keeping the clay in the palm of the hand maintains the rounded base until you are ready to form the shape at a later stage.
- Pinching inside the ball while leaving the rim quite thick and relatively closed will help prevent the shape from flaring out too quickly and stop the rim from tearing and cracking.

3 Pinch out the wall of the bowl in stages, first to one even thickness, then a little thinner. You may need to do this several times. Finally, pinch out the rim so that the form flares outwards from the base. Do not worry if the rim sways a little; this can be corrected later or left as a feature of the bowl.

TIP FOR DRYING
In general, pinching dries the clay quickly, especially if the maker has hot hands. However, if the bowl seems too floppy, this can be corrected by drying the clay out a little with a hair-dryer. Make sure you turn the bowl to avoid overdrying in one area, and only dry the bowl until it can be handled more readily.

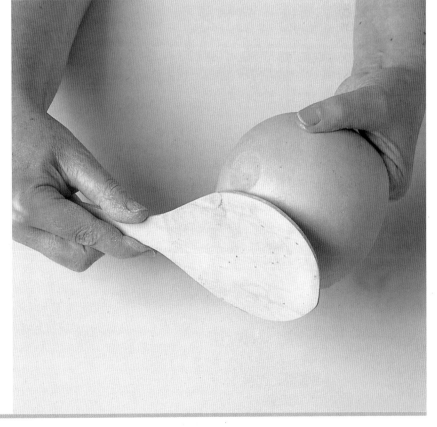

4 Turn the bowl over, hold it firmly in one hand, and then carefully paddle the outer wall with a wooden spatula to form a small base from which the rest of the shape flares. Use a flexible metal kidney to carefully scrape the inside and outside surfaces smooth of any irregularities. Leave the rim as it was pinched for an organic effect or level it off using a surform or a rasp blade before gently rounding off again with a rubber kidney.

ROLLING COILS

Coiling is one of the most traditional methods of constructing pots from clay. Rolling coils requires practice, however. It is worth taking the time to learn to do this well because evenly rolled coils build pots with walls of an even thickness. You can practise with any type of clay, as almost all are suitable for coiling.

1 Begin by forming the clay into a thick, rough coil shape between your hands. Ease out gently from the centre towards each end to form a manageable size for rolling. Try not to leave deep finger marks because this will cause problems when rolling. The coil should be as even as possible.

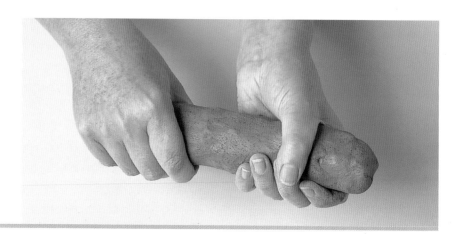

2 Lay the coil onto a clean, dry, nonabsorbent surface. Using your palms, roll the coil gently but firmly back and forth, beginning at the centre of the coil and working out towards each end. The final thickness of the coil depends on the type of pot. Practise rolling coils of varying sizes to begin with. Another good exercise is to roll multiples of a particular sized coil; this will help speed the construction process later.

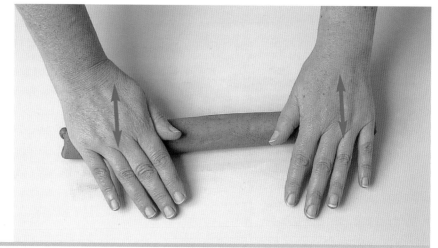

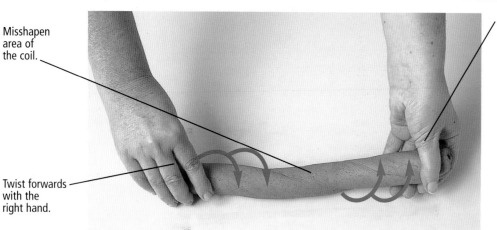

Misshapen area of the coil.

Twist forwards with the right hand.

Twist backwards with the left hand.

3 A common problem when rolling coils is that they tend to lose their shape in the rolling process. To correct the shape of the coil, hold it at each end and twist gently in opposite directions until it returns to a rounded shape; then re-roll to size. You can repeat this process as often as required.

ADAPTING ROUNDED COILS

Coils can be used in a rounded form or in a flattened version that speeds up the process a little and gives greater control over the thickness of the clay wall. In addition, less scraping back of the wall is required at a later stage because the wall is more uniform to begin with.

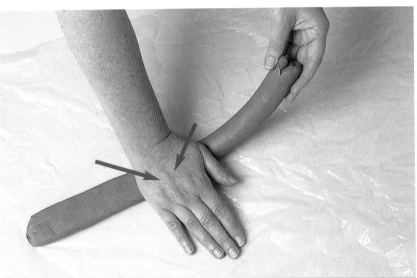

1 Form a thick rounded coil as described on page 24. Lay one end of the coil on a sheet of plastic while keeping the other end slightly raised. Use the heel of the other hand to flatten the coil along its length by applying firm and even pressure.

When you have worked along the length once, lift the coil off the plastic sheet, turn it over and repeat the process until it is the thickness you require.

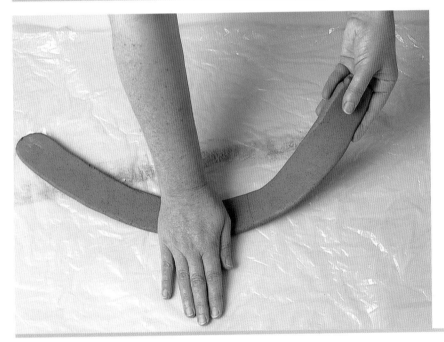

2 To help form the shape of a pot, flattened coils can be manipulated into a curved shape during the final part of the flattening process. The process is the same as for flattening straight except that you turn the coil gently as you press. Manipulating the coils in this way allows you to build the form in either an outwards or inwards direction.

TIP FOR COIL SHAPE

Do not make the coils less than 2.5 cm (1 in.) in diameter to begin with because this will make them difficult to handle. With practice you will find you can flatten the coils to about 6 mm (¼ in.) thick or possibly thinner but this may take some time to achieve. It is easy enough to scrape the walls back at a later stage if you feel they are too thick.

SEE ALSO:
Basic skills: *Rolling coils, page 24*

Technique 4: *Building with flattened coils, pages 62–63*

ROLLING SLABS

Slabbing is a very versatile technique that allows you to build forms from both hard and soft clay. There are certain basic rules for successful slabbing – most importantly the uniform thickness of the slabs. It is worth taking some time to practise rolling clay evenly if you want to avoid problems at the later stages of construction, or even at firing.

TIPS FOR SUCCESSFUL SLABBING
- To avoid air bubbles, always make sure that your clay has been very thoroughly wedged prior to rolling out.
- Form the lump of clay into a rough square shape to make rolling easier.
- If, in the process of rolling, you notice small air bubbles trapped in the clay, pierce them with a potter's pin. Roll over the surface again, making sure the guides are still in place to avoid altering the thickness of the slab.

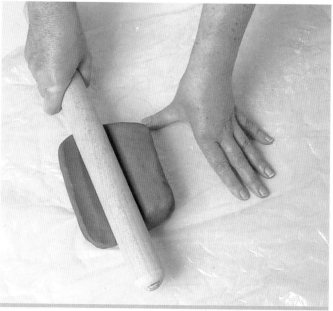

1 Lay the clay on a sheet of clean plastic. Using evenly weighted strokes, beat the clay with a rolling pin. Work systematically from one side of the block to the other. This helps reduce the initial bulk of the block of clay and drive out any air that may still be trapped in the clay.

Lift the block of clay off the plastic sheet. Turn it over and through 90 degrees. Repeat the process.

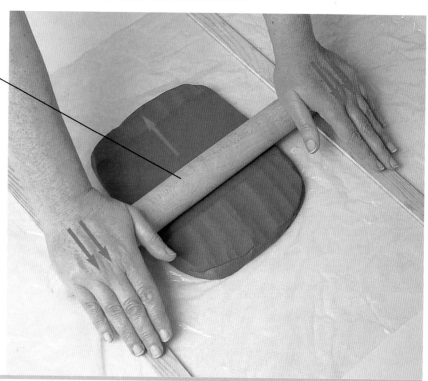

Keep an even pressure on the rolling pin.

2 Reposition the clay on the plastic sheet with a roller guide positioned on each side so that the ends of the rolling pin can rest on them to gauge the final thickness of the slab.

Position the pin in the middle of the block and then roll away from your body and back again. It will not be possible to roll the slab in one try. Roll until you feel a natural resistance to any further rolling. This is a good indication that the slab needs to be turned.

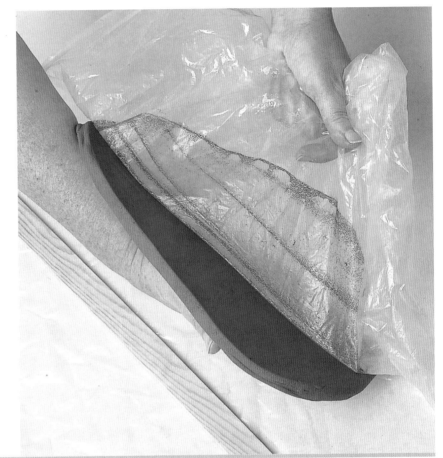

3 To turn the slab, lift it in place on the sheet of plastic. Turn it over to rest on the opposite hand. Very carefully peel the plastic off the back of the slab and replace it in position on the work surface.

It is very important to remove the plastic sheet in this way to avoid ripping or distorting the slab.

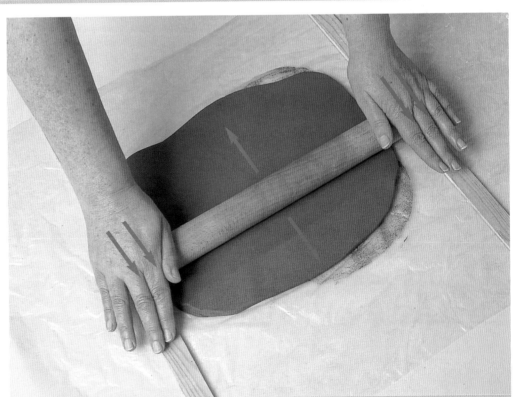

4 Rotate the slab 90 degrees, turn it over and replace it on the sheet. Reposition the roller guides and repeat the rolling process. You may need to lift and turn the slab several times. The slab will be ready when the pin rolls over the clay and the guides without meeting any resistance.

THROWING

Throwing is not necessarily a technique for absolute beginners because it requires the use of a wheel, which is an expensive piece of equipment. Also, to master the technique requires endless amounts of practice, with improvement often seeming to be very slow. However, once mastered, the technique is endlessly rewarding, as it allows you to produce a vast range of wares in a relatively short space of time. Perhaps the best time to start on the wheel is when you have learned (and are well practised in) the hand-building techniques and you are really hooked on clay!

CENTRING

Thoroughly knead a ball of clay weighing about 2.2 kg (1 lb) to remove trapped air and smooth out the consistency. Dampen the wheel head with a little water, but do not soak it, as this will prevent the clay from sticking and could even cause it to fly off when the wheel starts to turn.

Throw one of the clay balls down onto the centre of the wheel head and make sure that it is firmly in place. If you find you missed the centre, gently push the clay into place. Keep a bowl of water and a sponge close by in the wheel tray. Sprinkle a little of the water over the clay to get started. Sit close to the wheel head. Tuck your elbows into the side of your body, with your forearms resting on the side of the tray to lock them into position.

Use the fingers of your left hand to create a mushroom shape as you push the clay downwards and inwards.

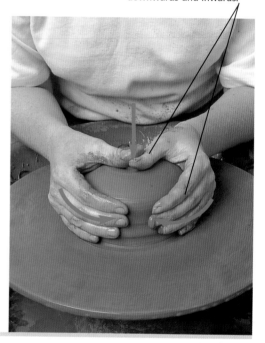

1 Once the wheel is moving, cup the clay with your hands and squeeze inwards using your thumbs on top of the clay to exert downwards pressure. Keep the thumbs together. Pull the clay ever so slightly towards the body to completely centre it.

Keep your fingers just above the wheel head to prevent chafing the skin on your little finger.

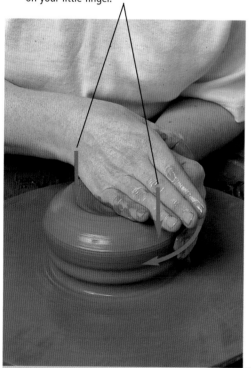

2 To level the clay lump and ready it for opening up, hold the left hand steady in a vertical position against the side of the clay mass. Use the side of the right hand, as shown, to exert downwards pressure on the clay through its centre. This forces the clay in an outwards direction. This secondary action smoothes out the clay as it widens, while forcing any wobbles to be incorporated into the clay mass as it rotates.

The clay should now be centred and ready for the next stage in the making process.

CONING UP

Coning up eliminates any unevenness in the clay. It should not be necessary if the clay has been prepared correctly in the first place. However, it is a good technique to learn as it helps align the particles in the clay into a spiral, which some potters say helps make the clay easier to throw.

Remember to keep the clay lubricated with a little water.

1 When the clay is centred, place both hands around its base and squeeze them together. As you squeeze, the clay will be forced upwards into a cone.

If you started with a wide base of clay, you will find that the walls pull up as you squeeze, leaving a well in the centre of the cone where water will gather. This will weaken the clay as it becomes incorporated. Avoid this problem by starting from a centred lump of clay that has not been widened too much.

It is important to keep your arms supported on the wheel tray as the cone gets taller because narrower forms are more likely to wobble.

2 Continue to squeeze the clay inwards and upwards as you move your hands up the cone. Overlap the fingers as the cone gets narrower to help hold the hands steady. Always take the hands away carefully to avoid knocking or jerking a form off centre again.

Exert downwards pressure with the right hand.

3 Hold the left hand firmly against the side of the cone. Place the side of the right hand on top of the cone and exert a downwards pressure. At the same time, push the cone slightly away from the body to keep the cone central.

The left hand prevents the wall from forming into a mushroom as it is forced downwards. If you allow the fingers of the right hand to touch those of the left hand, the clay has no room to displace out at the top of the cone. As a result, the cone becomes shorter and wider as it is forced down.

Repeat the coning up and down process two or three times until the clay is smooth and even.

The fingers of the right and left hand touch to prevent displacement of clay.

SEE ALSO:
Technique 7: *Throwing a bowl and plate, pages 74–79*

TURNING

Turning is the term used to describe the process of removing unwanted clay from a thrown form to refine and define its shape or to create a foot ring, which is a raised base on which the pot stands.

The clay must be leather hard to be turned successfully. That means stiff but still damp. However, every potter's idea of leather hard can be different, so you will have to practise to find the state of dryness that best suits you for turning. Here you will learn how to turn a basic foot ring on a bowl.

TIPS TO GET STARTED
- Dampen the wheel slightly with a sponge.
- Position the bowl upside down and centre it as best you can. Use the rings on the wheel surface as a guide. The bowl shown is positioned on a wooden bat (a device that extends the size of the wheel head) because its rim is wider than the wheel head. As a beginner, it is unlikely that your bowl will be as large as this.
- Support the pot with one finger on the base of the bowl. Gently tap the pot to the centre with the other hand at an 8 o'clock position. This may take a little practice but it is essential that the pot is properly centred before turning.
- Once the pot is centred, press it down gently onto the wheel to secure it.

1 Holding a ribbon tool in the right hand, rest the left hand on the pot with the thumb against the tool to keep it steady. With the wheel moving fairly swiftly, use the ribbon tool to remove excess clay from the width of the base.

Remove the clay from inside the foot using the ribbon tool at different angles to build up the ring. It is important not to make the width of the ring too thin because this will make it prone to damage. However, the size of the ring must be in proportion to the bowl.

2 Once you have achieved the width you desire, use the ribbon tool to define the outside shape of the ring. In this case, the edge is straight but you could round it off slightly if you prefer.

3 When you have trimmed away enough depth to form the ring, smooth the area inside the foot ring with a flat tool to remove any irregularities. The inner area of the foot ring should follow the inner curve of the bowl so that the clay wall is the same thickness throughout the bowl.

Remove the bowl carefully from the wheel head, and allow it to dry upside down.

SEE ALSO:
Technique 7: *Throwing a bowl and plate, pages 74–79*

MIXING PLASTER FOR MOULD MAKING

Plaster moulds can be incredibly useful to the potter who wants to be able to reproduce, quickly and accurately, a shape that cannot be easily made using hand-building or throwing methods. Making moulds can seem daunting to the beginner, but once you have learned how to mix the plaster you are halfway to mastering the technique.

Accurately weighing and measuring the plaster and water will ensure that you get the mix right the first time, but judging the amount required for a particular project takes practice. See below for weights and measures. Potter's plaster is widely available from ceramic suppliers.

PLASTER/WATER RATIO
675 g (1 ½ lb) plaster
575 ml (1 pint) water
This will give a strong mix for
most pottery uses.

1 Pour the measured water into a bucket or large bowl. Weigh out the required amount of plaster into another dry container.
   Carefully sprinkle the plaster powder into the water, adding it gradually and evenly until the powder breaks the surface of the water.
   Shake the bucket gently to make sure the plaster seeps down into the water. Allow the mixture to stand for a minute or two to allow the plaster to absorb the water fully.

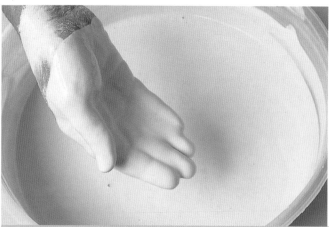

2 Stir the mixture gently with your hand to remove any lumps. Every so often, wiggle your hand at the bottom of the mixture to release any trapped air bubbles.
   If bubbles rise to the surface, scoop them off carefully with your hand and transfer them onto newspaper or, preferably, into a pre-lined bin, which will make disposal much easier later.
   Keep testing the viscosity of the mixture. When it no longer runs off your fingers, or is obviously thickening, it is ready.

SAFETY NOTE
- NEVER wash excess plaster down the sink as it will set in the pipe and cause a blockage.
- Wipe excess plaster from your hands with newspaper before washing them, again to avoid blockages.
- Use newspaper to clean out your plaster bucket immediately after use.
- Wear rubber or latex gloves to mix the plaster if your skin is sensitive.
- It is advisable to wear a face mask when mixing plaster if you are concerned about inhaling the dust.

COLOURING CLAY

Adding colour to clay can change its chemical make-up and reduce its plasticity. This can be overcome by making batches of coloured clays in advance and storing them for a couple of months before use. The best results are achieved by mixing metal oxides or commercially available stains into white clay, which allows for a brighter colour response.

Firing temperature is lowered by the addition of oxides and stains, so before using your coloured clay you should prefire a sample piece to test the colour response. Getting the right mix is a matter of trial and error.

This method of mixing colour into clay is perhaps the easiest, if a little messy, but an alternative would be to mix the colour into powdered clay prior to adding water and wedging.

1 Wearing your face mask and rubber gloves for protection, mix your chosen colourant with a little water to form a thick paste. Cut a block of white clay into slices, and spread the paste onto each layer as you pile them on top of one another.

2 Wedge the sandwiched clay and colour together several times using the wedging method described on page 16. You will find that the colour oozes out quite a bit as you do this but it can be kneaded back in at the next stage.

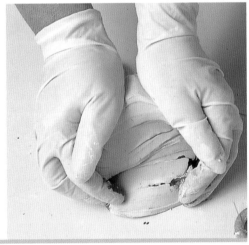

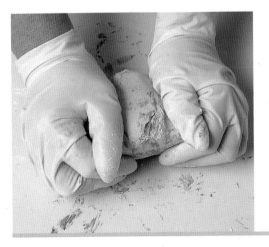

3 Finish the mixing process by kneading the clay, using the method described on page 17, until all the colour is thoroughly distributed.
   Store the coloured clay in an airtight bag for at least two weeks before use to restore its plasticity.

SAFETY NOTE
It is advisable to wear rubber gloves and a mask when handling oxides and stains in their dry state because they can be poisonous if inhaled or ingested, and some can be absorbed through the skin.

SEE ALSO:
Getting started: Clay, pages 16–17

Technique 12: Coloured clays, pages 104–105

DECORATING

One of the greatest pleasures of working with clay is decorating the surface, and there are countless methods of doing this. Some decoration is applied while the clay is still in a wet or leather-hard state, while other techniques require the clay to be bisque fired first. To practise, cut out a number of 15-cm (6-in.) squares from a slab of clay and make a few test tiles for each technique. Use different clays to see how this changes the effect and then bisque fire them for reference later.

CREATING TEXTURES

Almost anything can be used to make an impression in clay, and it is fun looking for things that will make an interesting mark.

STAMPS

These stamps are a mixture of found objects and handmade wooden, clay and plaster blocks. Try old earrings and buttons, shells, and wooden beading for interiors. Or make some stamps of your own design from clay and then bisque fire them.

You can use the stamps as individual motifs or use several together to create areas of pattern. Stamps are always best used on slabbed surfaces because the clay needs to be relatively soft.

ROLLING

These decorative plaster rollers are used in the interior decoration industry; they make wonderful impressions when rolled into clay. Similar effects can be achieved by wrapping string around a tube or stick. Or try carving patterns into short lengths of a wooden dowel or pole. You can also make clay rollers with impressed patterns to create continuous marks in pottery.

Rollers are best applied to flat surfaces prior to construction, but are often used to decorate the surface of thrown pots while they are still in a relatively soft state.

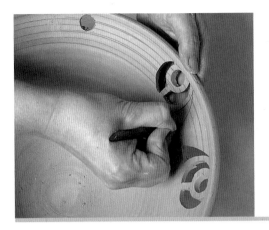

INCISING OR CUT OUT WORK

To cut sections away successfully, the clay must be leather hard. Place your pot on a banding wheel. Mark the lines between which you intend to cut the design with a potter's pin. Hold it firmly in one hand as you turn the wheel with the other. Lightly draw the design on the surface of the clay with accurate spacing.

Carefully cut away the sections with a sharp craft or other pointed knife. Support the clay wall with your other hand as you work. You can also use potter's hole-making tools, which come in several sizes, to start your design.

FABRICS

Rolling fabrics into clay is another wonderful method of decorating the surface. Here an old piece of crochet lace has been rolled into the clay. A yellow slip is painted over the surface before the lace is removed to define the pattern.

Almost all fabrics will make some impression in clay, although some will be more subtle than others. Look for samples in secondhand shops and markets; it can become quite an obsession!

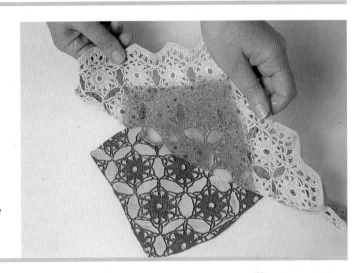

WALLPAPERS

Embossed wallpapers make similar impressions in clay as fabrics, but they have the added advantage that you can cut out shapes to form repeats if you want to create a particular effect.

Decorating shops often allow their customers to take away samples of paper, so try a few before buying a whole roll. Lay the paper on your slab with the roller guides still in place at each side. Roll over it carefully but firmly. Lift a corner of the paper with a pin to remove it.

ORGANIC MATERIAL

Try rolling leaves into the surface of the clay. Choose ones with interesting shapes or outlines, and preferably with distinct veining on the underside to make a good impression in the clay. Deciduous leaves are best because they are soft, but conifers can also make good marks. Some flowers work well, but try seed-heads, bark and seaweed as well.

APPLYING GLAZE

The main purpose of glaze is to make ceramics functional by forming a seal over the clay so that it becomes nonporous and hygienic to use. However, glaze is also another great method of decorating the surface of clay.

As a beginner, most of your efforts will be focused on learning how to make and build pottery, and it would be daunting to learn about the chemical composition of glazes. There is a fantastic range of commercially prepared glazes, available from pottery suppliers, which come in liquid or powder form. To prepare a commercial powder glaze, you need to add water and sieve the mixture through an 80, 100 or, occasionally, 120 mesh, according to the manufacturer's instructions. See pages 120–121 for glaze recipes.

TIP
Use a damp sponge to thoroughly wipe away any glaze from the surface on which the pot will sit in the kiln – otherwise your pot will seal onto the kiln shelf.

POURING
Fill a jug or similar container with glaze. Hold your pot over the glaze bucket as you pour the glaze over the surface. Do this in one action to avoid building up different thicknesses of glaze.

When glazing the undersides of larger items, suspend the pot upside down on two roller guides over a container that is large enough to collect the run-off glaze.

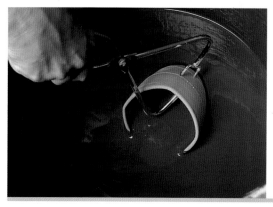

DIPPING
This is a quick method of glazing for the production potter who simply wants repeats of the same finish. As a beginner you are unlikely to have a large enough bucket of glaze to do this technique, but it may prove useful in the future.

To save time cleaning off the excess glaze, wax the base of your pots before dipping them. Hold your pot firmly in the tongs, dip it in the glaze quickly, and then pour out any excess. Do not leave the pot in the glaze for more than a couple of seconds or it will be too thick.

BRUSHING
Brushing glaze onto the surface of pots is more difficult than dipping because water from the glaze is quickly absorbed into the porous surface of the bisque clay. However, with some practice, you will be able to master the technique.

Place your pot on a banding wheel with your glaze bucket close by. Load your brush with glaze and apply it to the surface while rotating the wheel with the other hand. Repeat the process until the entire surface is covered evenly.

SLIP DECORATION

Slip is a term used to describe liquid clay, which can be coloured and used to decorate the surface of clay. Slip is one of the oldest methods of decoration and can be applied in any number of ways to create many different and expressive effects.

If you want to make coloured slips for decoration, it is best to use a white firing clay as a base; this can also be used as a simple white slip to cover dark clay bodies.

MIXING SLIP
To make a simple white slip, simply add water to powder ball clay a little at a time and mix until it forms a creamy consistency.

SIEVING SLIP
Pour the clay slip into an 80 mesh sieve suspended on roller guides over a bowl. Work the slip through the mesh using a rubber rib or a stiff bristle brush. If required, add small amounts of water afterwards to adjust the thickness. The slip should be the consistency of cream.

If the slip is too thin, allow it to stand overnight and then siphon off some of the water that will have settled on the surface.

ADDING COLOUR TO SLIP
Mix your chosen colourant with a small amount of water in a separate container to break down any lumps and disperse the colour properly. Pour the colour into the base slip through a mini 100–120 sieve with the help of a stiff bristle brush.

Mix the colour in well and then sieve the whole mixture through a 200 mesh sieve to prevent the colourant particles from speckling the slip.

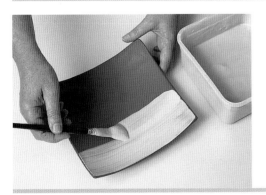

BRUSHING SLIP
Brush the slip onto the surface of your pot in even strokes with a soft brush. It may be necessary to apply several coats to cover a dark clay body. Allow each coat to touch dry before applying the next.

SEE ALSO
Surface decoration library: *pages 108–119*

Glaze recipes: *pages 120–121*

PAPER RESIST

This is a method of decorating that uses paper shapes to create a pattern or design on the surface of a pot – in much the same way as a stencil. The paper acts as a resist when coloured slip is applied over the surface, leaving the design in sharp outline when removed.

1 Cut out some shapes from newspaper to form the design on the surface of your pot. Dip the cutouts in water before applying them to the surface of the pot. Make sure the shapes are sealed down. If they are not, paint a little water over them and brush them flat.

TIP FOR PAPER RESIST

If you leave a small area of each paper shape exposed, you will easily be able to see them later when it is time to remove them.

2 Carefully sponge a coloured slip over the entire surface of the pot, including the paper shapes. Be careful that the shapes do not lift as you sponge because this will spoil the definition of the design. Allow the surface to dry off to the touch.

3 Using an open-textured natural sponge, apply a light third coat of coloured slip to the surface of the pot, allowing the colour underneath to show through.

Sponging slip onto the surface of a pot is yet another method of application that can be used to build up a flat layer of colour, or to create a multicoloured effect as shown here.

4 When the surface of the pot has dried to the touch, remove the paper cutouts. Use a potter's pin to avoid digging into the surface.

You could decorate the surface further with sgraffito, as shown on page 39, in the resist areas but there is always a danger of overworking a design. Sometimes less is more!

POURING SLIP

Pouring slip onto certain areas of a pot can give a lively base from which to build up a decorative surface using other techniques. It also forms a good contrast with the colour of the clay.

Here a leather-hard bowl is held over a large bucket while the slip is poured from a jug into the centre and allowed to run out. The process is repeated around the bowl to create a random striped effect.

MARBLING SLIP

Pour areas of contrasting coloured slips onto a press moulded dish (preferably while still in the mould). Shake the dish to move the colours around to form variegated patterns that look like marble. Don't shake the dish for too long or the colours will merge and look muddy. Carefully pour away any excess and wipe the edge clean.

SGRAFFITO

Sgraffito is a form of incising or drawing into clay. The technique is usually used on surfaces with a contrasting slip to the clay body so that when you cut through the slip the clay colour is revealed.

DIPPING SLIP

Providing you have a large enough bucket prepared, whole pots can be dipped in slip. Your pot will need to be on the dry side of leather hard because it will absorb a lot of water during this process. The method is particularly suited to forms that can be held inside, such as the cylinder shown here.

Supporting the form well, dip it quickly into the slip bucket up to the required point. Lift it out, allow it to drain over the bucket for a second or two and wipe away the excess from the base.

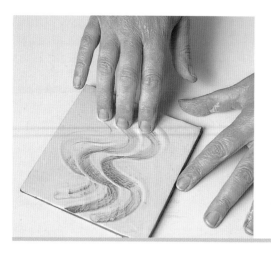

FINGER WIPING

This method of decorating a surface with slip is one of the most ancient. It provides a quick finish that shows the contrasting clay body colour underneath.

While the slip is still wet, simply draw your fingers through it to form a wavy pattern.

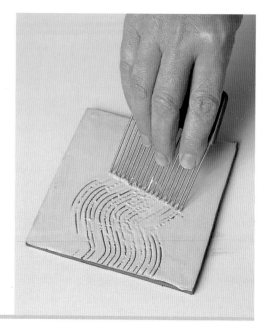

COMBING

You can use an old piece of wide-toothed comb, serrated plastic or rubber, or a kitchen device, like the one shown here, which is meant for holding onions while slicing.

Comb the lines through slightly damp slip to form a wavy pattern. Do not apply too much pressure, unless you want the extra effect of gouged lines in the clay.

INLAY

Inlaying is a versatile method of embedding contrasting coloured clays into the surface of a pot.

1 Here an incised pattern has been drawn onto the leather-hard surface. Now paint a contrasting coloured slip into the lines, as thickly as possible.

You may find that the slip shrinks into the lines as it dries, requiring another coat to build it up to the surface level.

2 When the inlay has dried to the leather-hard stage, carefully scrape away the excess slip with a metal kidney or scraper to reveal the inlaid pattern underneath.

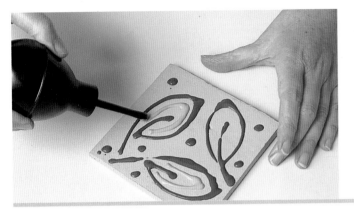

SLIP TRAILING

This is not an easy technique to master, and you may need some practice to perfect it, so begin on a flat or open surface.

Fill your slip-trailing bulb with fairly thick slip about the consistency of whipped cream. Squeeze the bulb in a consistent action as you draw out your design; this helps avoid spattering. Using both hands sometimes helps steady the technique. You may find it helpful to practise on sheets of paper until you are confident enough to work on clay.

FEATHERING

Feathering requires two or more bulbs of contrasting, coloured slip and is again best suited to a flat or open surface. The surface layer of slip needs to be very wet, so dip the pot into your chosen base colour of slip and then place it on the work surface or a wooden bat. Now slip trail lines of contrasting colours across the surface. The colours should appear to melt into the wet base slip.

Using a potter's pin or a feather quill, draw a series of lines in the same direction across the surface of the clay. Repeat the process in the opposite direction between the lines already drawn.

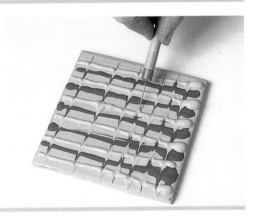

BURNISHING

Burnishing or polishing the surface of clay compacts the clay particles to create a shiny surface with some water resistance. It is the most ancient method of making pots functional and was widely used before the development of glaze. In modern times this technique is mostly used to create decorative surfaces that utilize the low firing effects of smoke or Raku. Some clay can be burnished directly. Red earthenware clay is particularly beautiful when burnished but others are too coarse to burnish well.

Various tools are used to burnish, from polished pebbles to old spoons. Whichever you choose, work over the surface in a circular motion to reduce the possibility of leaving marks. You may need to go over the surface several times. As the clay becomes smoother, you can complete the process by polishing the surface with a ball of absorbent cotton or a plastic bag stretched over a finger.

In this example, several coats of coloured slip were painted onto the surface and allowed to dry to leather hard to overcome any problems with the clay.

OXIDE DECORATION

Metal oxides are a traditional method of applying decoration to bisque-fired pots and can be used in several ways.

OXIDE ON TEXTURED SURFACE

Oxide can be used as a finish in its own right without the covering of glaze; it gives a rustic effect that is often suited to outdoor pieces. It is particularly good on texture, as it brings out the detail in the surface.

1 In this example, water is added to red iron oxide to form a thick emulsion. Paint the oxide onto the clay surface, making sure that all the texture detail is filled in.

2 Wear rubber gloves to sponge the oxide carefully away from the surface, but leave it in the texture patterning to sharply define the detail. The oxide will stay in all surface marks to add interest to the finished work.

PAINTED OXIDE ON BISQUE CLAY

Oxides can be used like paints to draw designs onto bisque-fired clay surfaces. This example shows a fine pattern of cobalt oxide being painted onto a tile, which will later be covered with a transparent or opaque glaze to soften the effect.

Mix the oxide with a little water to achieve a thin consistency for painting. Use a fine brush to paint oxides and try not to be too careful in the way you apply it. Be aware that cobalt oxide is quite strong, so a little will cover a large area. It need not be as thick as the last example; a simple wash will give good results.

SAFETY NOTE

Because of their toxic nature, oxides should not come into direct contact with skin. Wear rubber gloves to protect yourself.

PAINTED OXIDE ON GLAZE

Oxide can be painted directly onto a glazed surface, but this requires a slightly freer hand because the powdery glaze absorbs the oxide mixture very quickly, making it difficult to draw the brush across the surface.

A simple white tin glaze is used in this example, with cobalt oxide forming the decoration.

WAX RESIST

Wax for resist techniques can be bought in emulsion form from ceramic suppliers and applied with a paintbrush. Wash your brushes in very hot water after use to remove all the wax.

WAX RESIST UNDER GLAZE

Wax resist under glaze is a simple but effective technique that allows a pattern to be painted onto a bisque-fired surface, which prevents the glaze from being absorbed when applied. When the pot is fired, the wax burns away and the matt clay body colour is left in contrast to the shiny glaze (although you could equally well apply a dry firing glaze for effect).

WAX RESIST OVER GLAZE

The principle for this technique is almost the same as for the last, but the pattern is painted over a preglazed surface so that the base glaze colour will show through when subsequent glazes are applied over the top.

1 Begin by glazing your pot in a colour of your choice and then paint your design in wax emulsion over the top.

2 When the wax is dry, sponge another, contrasting glaze over the pattern to block out the base glaze colour.

TIPS

- You can use liquid latex instead of wax, with the added benefit that each layer can be removed after glaze application. This allows you to see more clearly how the design is building up.
- If you use latex, be sure to wash your brushes in boiling water after use; otherwise they will be ruined. A little detergent in the water also helps.

3 Apply some secondary wax detail to the surface to further enhance the finish.

4 Complete the surface by sponging a final coat of glaze in yet another colour on selected areas to correspond with the last wax detail.

SHELLAC RESIST

Strictly speaking, shellac is not a technique for beginners, but it creates such a lovely surface quality on fine clay, such as porcelain, that it is worth trying, even if only as a small detail.

You can buy shellac flakes from furniture makers and suppliers. Simply put the flakes in a screw-top container and cover with enough methylated spirits to form a slightly thickened liquid. It may take a while for the flakes to dissolve fully. Only make a small amount to begin with as a little goes quite a long way.

To practise this technique, it is best to roll out some slabs of porcelain and make a series of test tiles. Allow the tiles to dry out completely.

1 Draw your design onto the surface of the tile with a pencil, but do not make it too complicated; you will be surprised how good even the simplest designs can look when the tile has been fired. Now carefully paint the shellac inside the shapes you have drawn on the tile and allow to dry.

2 Using a damp natural sponge, carefully wipe away the clay from around the shellac pattern. Do not saturate the clay. If it appears to get too wet, allow it to dry thoroughly before wiping it again. The surface is finished when the area around the shellac pattern is considerably lower than the original thickness of the tile.

Allow the tile to dry again. Do not handle it too much because it will be quite thin and fragile now. The shellac will burn away when the tile is fired.

BRUSH ON GLAZES

A huge range of commercially prepared glazes is available from ceramic suppliers. The range extends from very low-firing decorative finishes through to high-fired glaze suitable for domestic use. Studio potters generally do not use these glazes because they can be quite expensive and are only available in relatively small containers. However, because you only need to purchase the smallest amounts, the beginner may find it interesting to try them.

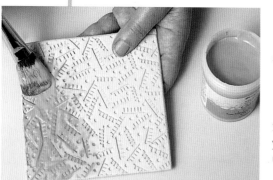

Simply choose your glazes from the ceramic catalogue and paint them onto your pots following the manufacturer's instructions. Several coats of glaze are usually required for a satisfactory result.

MAJOLICA

Majolica is the term used to describe the technique of painting colours over an unfired dry glaze surface. When fired, the colours melt into the glaze to fuse the design, which explains the technique's other name: in-glaze decoration.

Generally a white tin glaze is used as the base, although traditionally a transparent glaze would be applied over a white slip body. You could try both methods to see how they differ.

When tin glaze is used over red earthenware clay, it is commonly referred to as tin-glaze earthenware.

Mix some powdered underglaze colours with a small amount of glaze and a few drops of water to a paintlike consistency. Use a palette knife to mix the colours.

Glaze your surface with white tin glaze using one of the methods described on page 36 and allow to dry.

Apply large areas of colour with a soft bristle brush. Load the brush with colour to avoid running out mid-stroke because any mistakes will show up in the firing. Build up the design using more colours and different sized brushes for finer detail. You can also use an open-textured sponge to apply additional colour, or shaped sponges instead of brushes to create the design.

ENAMELS

Enamels are prepared colours composed of metal oxides and fluxes that are applied to previously fired glazes, and which melt at low temperatures to fuse onto the surface. The firing range for enamels is similar to lustre, but starts at around 650–780°C (1202–1400°F).

Enamels are the brightest of all ceramic colourants and are available from ceramic suppliers in a wide range of hues in either liquid or powder form. If you buy the powder variety, you will also need to purchase a special oil medium to mix the colour for application.

You can apply enamels with a brush or a sponge. In this example, small shaped sponges are used to build up a design. The enamel colours have been prepared on a tile in advance to make the application easier.

If you make a mistake when applying the enamel, simply wipe it off and begin again. It is important to fire enamels slowly to begin with, to allow the oil medium to burn off. If fired too fast, the oil will boil and bubbles will spoil the surface.

UNDERGLAZE APPLIED WITH SHAPED SPONGES

Underglaze colours are available in powder or liquid form; you can choose either type for this technique. If using powders, simply water down to a paintlike consistency before use. Shaped sponges are widely available from craft suppliers and some ceramic suppliers, but you can also make your own. Dampen a sponge and put it in the freezer for a while. Draw out your design on the frozen sponge and then cut it out using a sharp craft knife.

Underglaze design is usually applied directly onto a white bisque surface, which allows for the best colour response. If you have only red clay, you can apply several layers of white slip before firing to overcome the problem.

1 Prepare your colours on a plate or old tile surface ready for use. Dampen your shaped sponge. Load the sponge with colour by using a brush or simply by dipping it. The advantage of applying the colour with a brush is that you can be very specific about where the different colours are placed.

2 Sponge the design onto your chosen surface using gentle but firm pressure. Think about the positioning of the pattern and carry the design over the edges if appropriate. Reload the sponge when the pattern appears to be thinning too much.

3 Add finer details in a contrasting colour with a thin brush. Apply a transparent glaze over the design and fire to the required temperature.

LUSTRE

Precious metal lustre is quite an expensive treatment for clay and requires some practice to apply. Lustre colours are not quite so expensive and can be used for experimenting.

Lustre is usually used to highlight certain details on a ceramic surface as a final detail when the work has gone through all firing procedures. It can be applied over glaze for a shiny, lustrous effect or directly onto the fired clay body for a more subtle, matt finish.

The lustre is usually fired between 700–780°C (1292–1400°F); any higher and it will simply burn off.

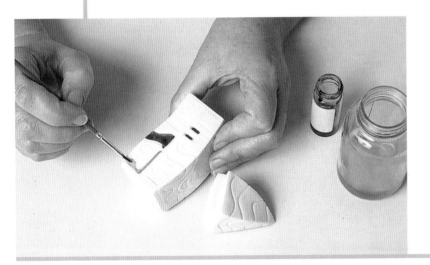

1 The problem with lustre is that it is quite sticky to apply and all colours are brown before firing, which can be very confusing. To overcome this, apply only one colour to all relevant areas at a time. Paint the lustre thinly but evenly in the required areas directly from the file container. Clean the brush after each use in lustre thinner (a liquid developed for thinning lustre when it has become too thick but also used for cleaning brushes) to avoid contaminating the colours.

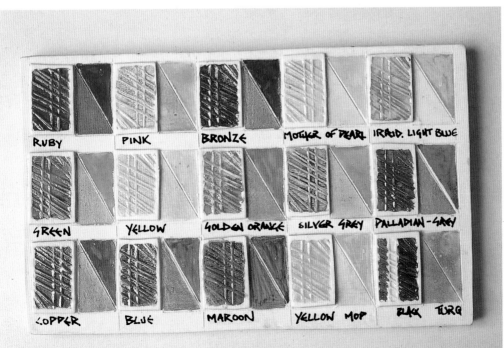

RUBY   PINK   BRONZE   MOTHER OF PEARL   IRRID. LIGHT BLUE

GREEN   YELLOW   GOLDEN ORANGE   SILVER GREY   PALLADIAN-GREY

COPPER   BLUE   MAROON   YELLOW MOP   BLACK TURQ

2 If you intend to use lustres regularly, it is a good idea to make a test tile of all the colours to show how they look on different surfaces.

This tile shows the range of lustre colours on a glazed surface in its shiny form, on an unglazed surface for the matt form and on texture for a quite different finish. The colour of each lustre is written underneath each sample for quick reference.

TECHNIQUES AND PROJECTS

There are really no definitive rules in pottery as there are in other craft disciplines. Each potter ultimately finds his or her own way of working with clay, which is usually an adaptation of techniques learned. However, there are some basic principles of clay construction that will help you to understand the material and get you started.

This section contains all the basic construction techniques you need to build your skills. Each technique is followed by a project that puts those new skills into practice. By the time you have worked your way through this section, you will know all the basics of pottery. From there, you will be able to develop your own unique style.

HAPPY POTTING!

PINCHING AND MODELLING

In this technique you will learn how to pinch shapes to fit together and how to make different sized and shaped pots that can then be used to form details, such as feet and lids.

You may need to practise pinching some of the smaller sections demonstrated because they can be quite tricky at first, but they have so many uses that it is worth taking the time to get this technique right.

1 It is much easier to pinch equal-sized pots if you weigh your clay beforehand. A good starting point would be two 90 g (3 oz) balls of clay. Pinch the first ball out to form a cup shape. When pinching the second ball of clay, measure the two halves regularly to check that the rims are the same size.

If the rims do not fit together well, or if the clay is cracked, you can use a surform blade to level them before joining the two pots together.

2 Pinching very tiny amounts of clay can be quite tricky, especially if you have big hands. A neat way of getting around the problem is to use the little finger (instead of the thumb or forefinger) to pinch out the shape from the inside.

You will need to support tiny balls of clay in the fingers, rather than in the palm of the hand, while pinching, in order to keep the shape. Such small pinched shapes have all sorts of uses as feet, lids, handles or even surface decoration.

TIPS FOR SUCCESS

- Cut your fingernails. Pinching clay is almost impossible with long nails.
- Use freshly wedged clay for each section you pinch so that the outer surface does not have time to dry out.
- Grogged clay is good for beginners because it holds its shape more readily than finely particled clays.

- Hot hands will dry the clay much faster than cool hands. You can keep them cool by running them under a cold tap from time to time.
- If the rim of your pinch pot cracks, stroke the clay from either side over the rim to seal it up.

3 OTHER SHAPES Not all pinched forms have to be round and open; it is quite possible to pinch different shapes. However, it is still very important that the thickness of the clay wall is as even as you can make it.

To pinch out a cone shape, make your ball of clay roughly cone shaped before you begin. Once the cone has been formed, press the finger or thumb through the clay mass to the pointed end of the cone. Pinch and smooth the clay backwards, away from the end of the finger, turning the shape regularly as you work.

Cone-shaped pinch pots can also be used for feet and are useful as decorative lids.

Smooth the coil with a modelling tool.

4 JOINING To join pinched sections together, score and slip the rims using a toothbrush and a little water. Join the sections together, making sure the fit is good, and hold them in place for a second or two until the rims bond properly.

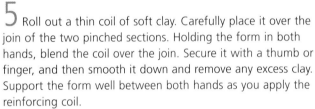

5 Roll out a thin coil of soft clay. Carefully place it over the join of the two pinched sections. Holding the form in both hands, blend the coil over the join. Secure it with a thumb or finger, and then smooth it down and remove any excess clay. Support the form well between both hands as you apply the reinforcing coil.

You will now have a form that looks rather like a dinosaur egg. This is a very versatile shape from which you can make any number of forms, such as fruits, pods, animals, birds, bottles, jars and vases.

6 Before modelling or further developing the shape of the pinched form, it may help to firm up the clay a little with a hair-dryer. Dry to a stage somewhere just short of leather hard.

You can manipulate the shape of the joined pinched sections only after releasing some air from the form by piercing one end with a potter's pin. Here, the shape is formed by squeezing the clay wall between the finger and thumb while supporting it in the palm of the hand. When the first two grooves are complete, model a third groove to create a vegetable or pod shape. If you think you have released enough air to prevent the shape from collapsing while it is being refined, fill in the hole with a small coil of clay.

SEE ALSO
Basic skills: *Pinching to make a simple bowl, page 22*

LIDDED PINCH POT

In this project you will put together all the skills you have learned so far to make a pinched bottle with a lid and quirky modelled details. Any clay is suitable for this technique, but here a white grogged clay with a wide firing range is used in order to maximize the colour response from the decorative slips.

The finished pot was decorated using paper resist with coloured slips and sgraffito detail. Once bisque fired the pot was covered in transparent glaze and fired to 1080°C (1976°F) in an electric kiln. Details on the lid and handles were painted with copper lustre and fired again to 730°C (1342°F).

YOU WILL NEED

MATERIALS
White grogged clay

FOR DECORATION
Slip
Coloured slips

TOOLS
Metal kidney
Hair-dryer
Wooden spatula
Toothbrush
Potter's knife
Metal modelling tool
Wooden modelling tool

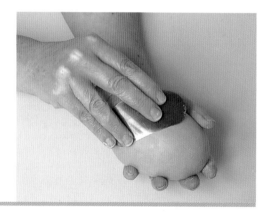

1 Weigh two 115 g (4 oz) balls of clay and pinch out the shapes equally. Join the halves and reinforce the seam with a coil of soft clay. Carefully refine the surface with a flexible metal kidney to remove any lumps and bumps. As an alternative, you can refine the surface of the pot by paddling it gently with a wooden spatula.

Keep multiples of a shape and size close by to make sure you pinch each one out to the same size.

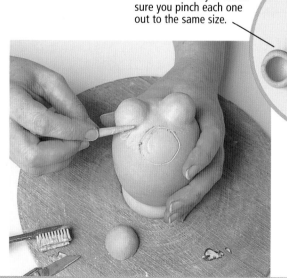

2 **PINCHING THE FEET** Pinch out three tiny, equal-sized balls of clay. Roll a thick coil of soft clay and form it into a ring on which to support the pot while you apply the feet. Place the feet on the bottom of the pot so that they are spaced equally. Gently score around each one to mark their positions. Using a toothbrush, score and slip the marked positions and the rims of the feet. Fix the feet onto the surface. Carefully blend the clay around each foot with a modelling tool. Finish by smoothing with a finger.

The fingers of one hand support the pinched section to maintain control of the shape as it is pinched.

• The forefinger and thumb carefully pinch out the tiny shape after the little finger has formed the opening.

3 **CREATING THE LID** Pinch out a cone-shaped lid; 60 g (2 oz) of clay will be sufficient. Stand the pot on its feet. Place the lid on top to measure the size of the opening. Gently score around the rim of the lid to mark the position. Using a potter's knife, cut out a hole about 6 mm (¼ in.) smaller than the marked size of the lid.

Make the coil that forms the rim quite thick to begin with. This will allow plenty of room for making adjustments later. It is easier to take surplus clay away than to add back on if the rim is too thin.

Use both hands to place the coil rim to avoid distorting the shape.

4 Roll out a coil of soft clay. Form it into a ring after measuring the size around the opening of the pot. Carefully blend the clay over the seam, trying not to distort the shape. Score and slip the area around the opening on the pot and the corresponding surface on the ring.

Fix the ring into place on the pot. Blend it into place with a modelling tool. Check that the lid will fit over the ring. Blend the inside of the ring around the opening with a wooden tool. Carefully level off the new opening without removing too much clay.

• Have the lid close by to check the fit as you secure the coil rim to the body.

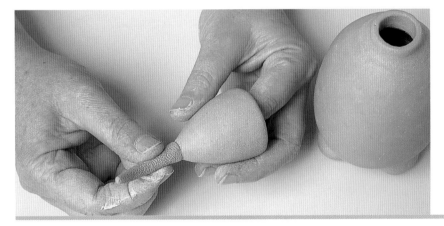

5 Roll out another small coil of clay into a conical shape that is slightly thinner at one end than at the other.

Cut the coil cone to a suitable size to form a handle on the lid of the pot. Score and slip the surfaces to be joined and fix the coil into place. Neaten around the join with a fine modelling tool, and then bend the coil very slightly to give it a jaunty angle.

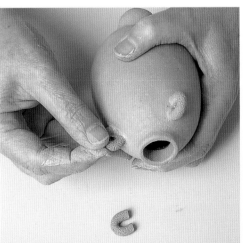

6 **MAKING THE HANDLES** Roll another thin, but even, coil of clay and texture it in the same way as for the handle on the lid. Cut three small, equal lengths of the coil and curve each one carefully into a U shape. Mark the positions for the tiny handles on the pot, just below the lid. Take care to space them equally.

Score and slip all surfaces to be joined. Fix the handles onto the pot, and neaten the joins carefully to remove any excess slip. The pot is now ready for decoration.

SEE ALSO

Basic skills: *Pinching to make a simple bowl, pages 22–23*
Decorating: *Paper resist, page 38*

Techniques: *Pinching and modelling, pages 50–51*
Glaze recipes: *pages 120–121*

PINCHING LARGE SECTIONS

Pinching larger lumps of clay to fit together can be just as difficult to master as tiny amounts. Although the basic skill is the same, you need to understand how the clay will behave in order to control the shape. The process will, of course, take longer, and you may need to allow the clay to firm up at various stages of pinching in order to prevent collapse. However, practice and patience will help you achieve good results.

1 It is possible to join sections that have been pinched in two different shapes by making your lumps of wedged clay into roughly the shape you want them to be when completed before you start to pinch.

Each of these balls of clay weighs 230 g (8 oz). One has been formed into a ball to open out to a cup shape, while the other is slightly conical to make a longer section.

It is important to pinch the base first because, once the sides begin to open and grow, it will not be possible for your fingers and thumb to reach down to the base to pinch it out further.

Turn the ball regularly as you pinch evenly.

2 **PINCHING** Hold the first ball of clay in the palm of one hand. Press the thumb down through the centre of the clay to the base. With your thumb fully immersed in the clay, continue to pinch out the bottom of the ball only. Try not to open out the form too much to begin with.

3 Use a hair-dryer to firm the clay, if required, while turning the section in your hand. Now start to pinch out the form again, remembering to smooth over any tiny cracks that may appear on the surface.

Aim to pinch out the shape until the wall is about 6 mm (¼ in.) thick. Any thinner and you risk the form cracking seriously when it is manipulated later. Do not worry if this is too thin for you to manage at first; a thicker wall will not be a problem, providing it is evenly pinched. Variations in thickness of the clay wall can create stresses when the pot is fired, which can cause the pot to crack.

4 **CONICAL SHAPES** Pinching larger conical shapes can be difficult because you can only pinch as far as your fingers will reach. Pinch open the shape just sufficiently to get your hand inside. With your hand inside the form and your longest finger at the bottom, manipulate the clay in a pinching/smoothing action over the tip of your finger with the fingers of your other hand. There should not be a mass of clay at the end of the cone.

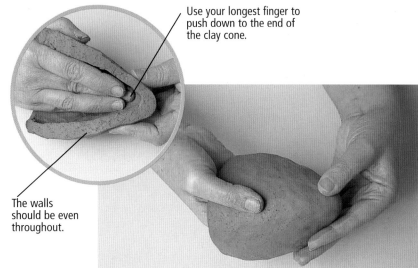

Use your longest finger to push down to the end of the clay cone.

The walls should be even throughout.

5 Firm up the clay cone a little with a hair-dryer if it feels too floppy, and measure the opening regularly against the opening of the first form to get the correct fit. Continue to pinch the shape, so that the thickness of the wall matches that of the previous section.

6 **JOINING** Score and slip the rims of both pinched sections. Join the sections and hold them together for a minute or two for the clay to bond.

Roll a coil of very soft clay and reinforce the join as described on page 51. Hold the sections together very firmly to reinforce such a large form.

Sit the form on your worktop. While pushing the sections together, work around the seam, using both thumbs to blend in the coil. Finish by smoothing the form with a metal kidney to remove any lumps and further reinforce the seam.

SEE ALSO
Basic skills: *Pinching to make a simple bowl,* pages 22–23

PINCHED PEBBLE PLANTER

This project puts together all the pinching techniques you have learned so far, and introduces an inlay decoration that is slightly different from the method on page 40. Here, clay coils are used instead of slip to fill the sgraffito pattern lines.

You will need two colours of clay. It is best to choose clays with a matching firing temperature for a good fit and to avoid differences in shrinkage rate. Red and white earthenware would be a good colour contrast, but they do not vitrify in firing and, therefore, would not be waterproof. The best choice is coarse, groggy stoneware clay and a white firing clay. You can add additional colour later, in the form of an oxide wash.

The finished pot was bisque fired to 1000°C (1832°F). A wax resist was painted over the inlaid lines. The body was then decorated with a manganese dioxide wash. The pebble was fired to 1260°C (2300°F) in an electric kiln.

Pierce the hole in a suitable position. Do not make the hole in an area that is to be manipulated a lot because the clay will distort and close the hole up again.

•To avoid impressing the clay with finger marks, support the shape carefully in the palm of the hand as the hole is pierced.

Use a potter's pin to release air from the enclosed pot.

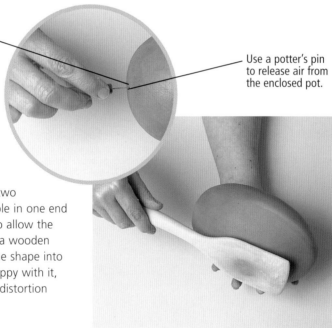

YOU WILL NEED
MATERIALS
Coarse, groggy
  stoneware clay
White firing clay

FOR DECORATION
Oxide wash

TOOLS
Potter's pin
Wooden spatula
Wooden modelling tool,
  or loop tool
Thin paintbrush
Hair-dryer
Rubber kidney
Onion fork or comb
Craft or potter's knife

1 Pinch out and join together two 230 g (8 oz) sections. Make a hole in one end of the form with a potter's pin to allow the shape to be manipulated. Using a wooden spatula, gently but firmly beat the shape into a pebble form. When you are happy with it, plug the hole to prevent further distortion in handling.

2 SURFACE DECORATION Sit the pebble on your work surface and consider its shape. Turn it around several times to figure out where best to apply the inlaid lines.

Score your sgraffito lines or grooves into the pebble with a wooden modelling tool or a small loop tool. Take care to score the lines or grooves deep and wide enough to apply the inlay, but not so deep that you pierce the wall.

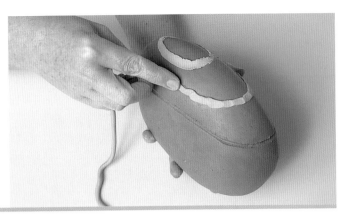

3 Roll out a thin coil of soft clay in a contrasting colour. Using a thin paintbrush and water, moisten the clay in the groove of the pebble and very carefully press the coil into place with a finger. Fill all the grooves in the same way. Work back around each one to make sure that the clay fills the space.

Set the pebble to one side to allow the clay to firm up to leather hard, or use a hair-dryer to speed up the process.

4 When the pebble has dried enough, carefully scrape away the excess clay from the inlaid lines. If the clay drags, it is still too wet to work on. Dry the form off a little more with the dryer and try again. The inlaid lines should be clean and sharp when finished.

The opening is off-centre to maximize the effect of the inlaid decoration.

• Score around the kidney with a wooden tool before cutting out the shape. This allows you to change your mind if the opening is too big or not quite right in some way.

5 **CREATING THE OPENING** Roughly score the position of the opening for your planter. You can do this freehand or by drawing around something suitable.

Now very carefully texture the clay of the pebble, taking care to work around the inlaid lines. Here, an onion fork is used. Score in a cross-hatch action and then gently paddle the roughness back down again.

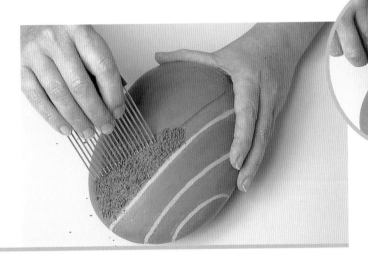

The rubber kidney makes a perfect shape for the opening of the pebble because it reflects the shape.

Save money by using everyday kitchen utensils, such as a wooden spatula, for paddling the surface of your pots.

6 When the whole surface has been textured, carefully cut out the previously marked opening with a craft or potter's knife and neaten around it. If you can get your hand, or a tool, inside the pebble, smooth over the seam where the pinched halves were originally joined. This isn't essential because the seam won't be seen, but it is good practice to finish your pots to the best of your ability, both outside and (where possible) inside.

Scoring the clay in this way can make it very rough to the touch. Paddle over the surface once you have finished texturing to give a more natural finish.

SEE ALSO
Decoration: *Inlay, page 40; Oxide decoration, page 42*

Techniques: *Pinching and modelling, pages 50–51*

USING ROUNDED COILS

Coiling allows you to form virtually any shape to any size, depending on the kiln available. Most clay is suitable as long as it is fairly plastic. Smooth clay will benefit from a 20–30 per cent addition of grog or sand to increase its strength. This is especially important for larger pots.

It will speed up construction if you roll out your coils in advance, but you must store them under plastic to prevent them from drying out.

1 **FORMING A BASE** Roll out a small slab of clay using the method on page 26. Alternatively, flatten a small disk of clay with the heel of the hand on a wooden bat and then cut out a circle. Do not make the disk smaller than 4 cm (1½ in.) in diameter as it will be further reduced when you add the first coil.

TIPS FOR SUCCESS
- To build a vertical wall each coil should be positioned directly on top of the previous one.
- To flare the form outwards the coil should be positioned on the outer edge of the previous one.
- To bring the shape inwards the coil should be positioned on the inner edge of the previous one.

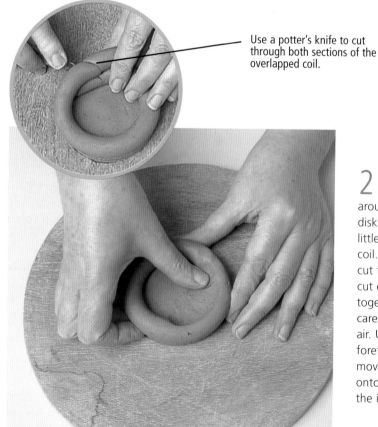

Use a potter's knife to cut through both sections of the overlapped coil.

2 **FIRST COIL** Score and slip around the edge of the base disk with a toothbrush and a little water. Position the first coil. Overlap the ends and cut through them. Join the cut ends of the coil back together and blend them in carefully to avoid trapping air. Using a thumb or forefinger in a downwards movement, blend the coil onto the clay base on the inside.

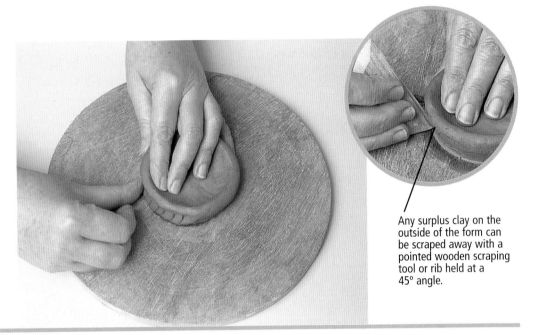

3 Carefully holding the base section in place with one hand, use a thumb or finger to blend the coil in around the edge. When the coil is thoroughly blended onto the base, develop an outwards flare on which to build the next coil.

Any surplus clay on the outside of the form can be scraped away with a pointed wooden scraping tool or rib held at a 45° angle.

4 FORM AND SHAPE To maintain the outwards flare, position each coil on the outer edge of the previous coil. The clay should be soft enough to allow you to add coils without having to score and slip. Each coil should be blended in thoroughly as before. Work systematically around the inner and outer edges of the pot, while the other hand supports the shape.

If the clay gets floppy, firm it up with a hair-dryer until it maintains its shape.

5 To shape the pot inwards, position a coil on the inner edge of the previous one and blend them together as before. To prevent distortion, take extra care to support the inner wall as you blend the coil on the outside. As the form closes, use a wooden modelling tool to blend the coils on the inside.

While you are still able to get your hand inside the pot, scrape away any surplus clay with a metal kidney. You can scrape back the outer wall when the pot is complete.

SEE ALSO
Basic skills: *Rolling coils, pages 24–25*

COILED VESSEL

In this project you will put the techniques on pages 58–59 into practice, as well as learn how to incorporate coils to form decorative detail. Working with coils in this way is a little more difficult and requires extra care when blending together on the inside, but the effect is exciting and opens up many possibilities for future designs.

After bisque firing to 1000°C (1832°F) a mixed oxide wash was sponged over the entire surface. The decorative rim and interior of the vessel were covered in dolomite glaze, which was sponged on in several layers. The vessel was fired to 1260°C (2300°F) in an electric kiln.

YOU WILL NEED

MATERIALS
Clay: grogged, buff stoneware
Cardboard, or a similar material
Paper

FOR DECORATION
Serrated kidney

TOOLS
Craft knife
Hair-dryer
Banding wheel
Wooden bat
Potter's knife or pointed modelling tool
Knife or surform blade
Pencil
Pastry cutter or bottle cap
Toothbrush
Metal kidney

Use your template as a guide to keep the correct shape.

1 **USING A TEMPLATE** Cut a template of the outline shape from rigid cardboard. Roll enough coils to allow you to build up the wall considerably. Form a base about 10 cm (4 in.) in diameter and build the form in an outwards direction until it measures about 35 cm (14 in.) in diameter.

Change the position of the coils so that the form builds inwards until the diameter of the opening measures about 25 cm (10 in.).

2 **CREATING THE RIM** Firm the clay up slightly at the rim of the pot with a hair-dryer. It will help if you rotate the pot on a banding wheel as you dry it.

Position a wooden bat, or any other round object, centrally on top of the vessel. Carefully score around the edge with a potter's knife or pointed modelling tool. Remove the bat. Trim the excess clay from inside the marked area with a knife or a surform blade to create a perfectly round rim.

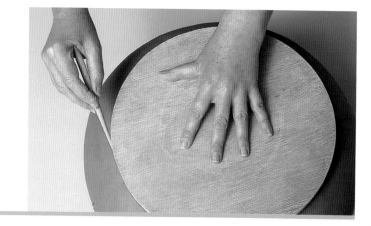

To carefully mark the position of each segment at the rim, place the folded paper over the opening.

3 Fold a sheet of paper cut to the same size as the bat four times to divide the circle into eight. Use it to mark the rim. Use a bottle cap or straight pastry cutter to mark out eight semicircles no more than 2.5 cm (1 in.) wide. Carefully cut out the shapes.

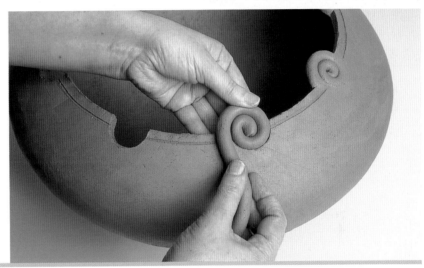

4 **Decoration** Roll a coil into a tight curl that will fit into a semicircle on the rim. Neatly cut away the excess coil where it meets the rim. Remove the coil and make seven more the exact same size, measuring each one against the first for accuracy.

Score and slip a semicircle edge with a toothbrush and a little water and carefully reposition the coil. Blend it into the main body of the vessel on the inside only, while supporting the coil on the outside.

The body can be textured with a serrated kidney in a cross-hatch action. Take care not to damage the decorative coils.

5 When all the curls are in place, fill in the spaces between them with sections of straight coil. Finish off with one long coil over the top. Make sure you blend the ends together neatly. Blend the coils on the inside and scrape away any irregularities with a metal kidney.

See also
Basic skills: *Rolling coils, page 24*
Decoration: *Oxide decoration, page 42*
Glaze recipes: *pages 120–121*

Technique 4 BUILDING WITH
FLATTENED COILS

Constructing forms from flattened coils is a little more difficult than using rounded coils. However, once you have mastered the technique, you will find that you can build up the form much faster and keep better control over the thickness of the clay wall. It is best to use a well-grogged clay.

1 FIRST COIL Roll out a coil about 4 cm (1½ in.) in diameter and flatten it in a curve as shown on page 25. On a wooden bat, cut out a circular base section from either a rolled slab of clay or clay that has been flattened by the heel of the hand. The base should be 6 mm (¼ in.) wider than the intended finished size.

Score and slip around the edge of the base with a toothbrush and a little water. For an outwards flare, position the inner curve of the coil 6 mm (¼ in.) in from the edge. Hold it in place for a second or two to make sure that it is secure.

2 REINFORCING THE BASE Overlap the coil. Cut through both ends diagonally so that they wedge together exactly when rejoined. Blend the ends together well, taking care not to trap air in the join.

Put the bat on a banding wheel. Use a wooden modelling tool to carefully blend the excess clay from the base up and over the coil. Work around the edge methodically, supporting the inner wall with your other hand.

TIPS FOR SUCCESS
- To prevent distortion of the shape, always support the wall of the pot with one hand as you work on the opposite side.
- Firm the clay up a little from time to time with a hair-dryer to prevent the clay from collapsing as the form gets bigger.
- Scrape away excess clay at regular intervals both inside and out so that you can stay in control of the developing shape.

Use a surform blade to level the rim of each coil.

3 Roll out a thin coil of soft clay and position it around the inside base. Blend the coil into the base and up the side of the flattened coil with a finger or a wooden modelling tool. It is important that the coil is fixed securely onto the base, so blend it well. To make construction easier, level the rim of the first coil before adding the next one.

4 **JOINS** Score and slip the rim of the first coil. Position the inner curve of the second coil onto the rim, making sure that it is secure. Overlap the coil ends and cut through them both diagonally. Blend the ends together carefully, taking care not to trap air or distort the shape.

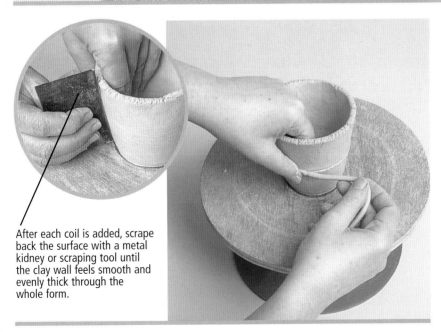

After each coil is added, scrape back the surface with a metal kidney or scraping tool until the clay wall feels smooth and evenly thick through the whole form.

5 Reinforce the join inside and outside with thin coils of soft clay. It does not matter which side you do first. Gently squeeze the reinforcing coil into the join with a thumb, working it in methodically as you rotate the pot. Support the wall with your other hand as you work.

When the coil is in place, blend it in further with a modelling tool, removing any excess clay in the process.

SEE ALSO
Basic skills: *Rolling coils, pages 24–25*

COILED VASE

This project combines the flattened coil method of construction with stencilled slip decoration and burnishing. Deciding when to burnish stencilled slip patterns can be tricky. If it is not done at the correct stage, the sharpness of the stencilled outline will be spoiled. If you are a beginner, it is a good idea to practise the decorating technique on test tiles before starting.

The vase was burnished to a high sheen before bisque firing to 960°C (1750°F). Wax polish was applied to the vase after firing to seal the surface and enhance the shine.

YOU WILL NEED

MATERIALS
Clay: grogged white
    firing clay
Paper

DECORATION
Slip: brown, yellow, blue
Soft brush or sponge
Newspaper stencil
Hair-dryer
Pebble or spoon
Potter's pin
Soft cotton glove

TOOLS
Roller guides
Craft knife
Spatula
Metal kidney
Surform blade
Rubber kidney

1 **GETTING STARTED** Roll out a slab of clay using 6–13 mm (¼–½ in.) roller guides. Cut out an oval-shaped base section of about 15 x 8 cm (6 x 3 in.). It helps to cut around a paper template of the base shape.
   Position a straight, flattened coil on the base. Reinforce it inside and out as demonstrated on pages 62–63.

2 **CREATING THE SHAPE** Continue to build the form up vertically, reinforcing the joins inside and out, until it measures 20 cm (8 in.) high. Position the next coil on the rim. Before you reinforce it, cut out a wedge of clay from both rounded ends of the form about 13 mm (½ in.) wide at the top and tapering to a point. Join the cut sections together, making sure the clay is well blended. Reinforce the coil as before.

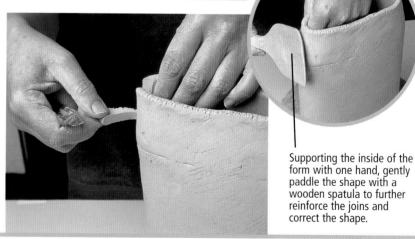

Supporting the inside of the form with one hand, gently paddle the shape with a wooden spatula to further reinforce the joins and correct the shape.

TIPS FOR SUCCESS

- Cut out the positive shape of your design in a stiff paper. Fix it to the newspaper with spray mount glue. Using the positive shape as a template makes it easier to cut out the newspaper stencil and allows you to repeat the design.

- Finger marks are easily transferred to the clay surface during burnishing. This can be avoided if you wear a soft cotton glove when you handle the pot.

3 The next two coils should be joined and cut in the same way to close in the neck of the vase until it measures about 8 cm (3 in.) wide and 2.5 cm (1 in.) from back to front.

Work over the surface with a metal kidney to remove any lumps and bumps. Remove scratches and marks by holding the kidney on its side and smoothing over the clay. Use a surform to level and neaten the rim. Soften the edges with a rubber kidney.

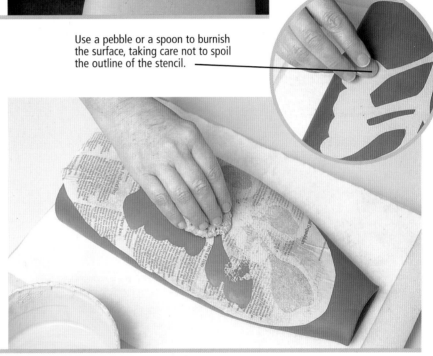

Use a pebble or a spoon to burnish the surface, taking care not to spoil the outline of the stencil.

4 **DECORATING THE SURFACE** Apply three coats of base colour slip to the surface with a soft brush or a sponge. Each layer should be dry to the touch before you apply the next. Cut out a stencil of your design from newspaper and lay it over the surface. Secure it in place by brushing it with a little water.

Using a contrasting colour and a natural sponge, apply three coats of slip to the stencil design. Dry each layer with a hair-dryer before applying the next. When the slip is dry to the touch, remove the paper stencil.

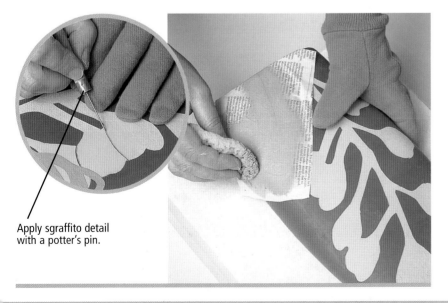

Apply sgraffito detail with a potter's pin.

5 Cut out another stencil design that will complement the first one. Fix the stencil in place as before. Sponge on three coats of another slip colour. Remove the paper and burnish the stencil carefully. You can continue to build up the design in this way with as many different colours as you choose. Finally, burnish the whole vase again until it is really smooth and shiny.

SEE ALSO
Basic skills: *Rolling coils, pages 24–25*

Decorating: *Burnishing, page 41; Paper resist, page 38; Sgraffito, page 39*

Building with firm slabs

This technique shows you how to construct forms from firm slabs of clay. It is not difficult, but to get good results you need to pay close attention to detail and finish. It is also important to cut the sections out accurately to avoid distortion of the shape.

Roll the slabs as demonstrated on pages 26–27. Let them dry on a wooden board to the leather-hard stage, turning them from time to time so they dry evenly.

You can use almost any clay for slabbing, so your choice should be governed by the surface finish.

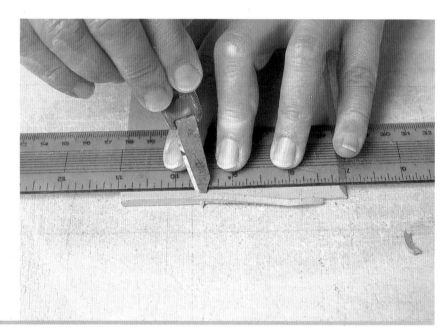

1 **MITRED JOINS** One method of joining slabbed edges together involves cutting the edges at a 45° angle to form a mitre. Cut out five equal-sized squares of clay to make a simple box.

Position a ruler 6 mm (¼ in.) in from the edge of the slab. Hold a craft knife so that its tip is on the board and the blade is on the ruler. Cut the mitre from the left to the centre. Turn the blade around and cut from the right edge back to the same point. Cutting in this way prevents the corners from breaking off.

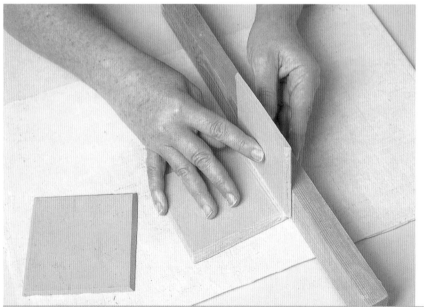

2 Mitre four sides of the base section and three sides of each other slab. Score and slip one mitred edge of the base section and the bottom mitred edge of a side section with a toothbrush and a little water. Fit them together. Hold the side in place for a second or two so the surfaces bond.

You can use a block of wood to hold the sections in place while you prepare the next one.

Support the walls with your other hand as you work along the seam.

After each section has been reinforced on the inside, straighten up the angle on the outside with a metal kidney or scraping tool.

3 Roll out a coil of soft clay and reinforce the inner joins, using a finger to blend the clay in. It is important to work the clay into the angle of the join thoroughly without trapping air in the seam. Do not apply too much pressure because this will push the sections apart again. A round-ended modelling tool will help to neaten the seam further. Add the remaining three sections in the same way.

4 **BUTT-ENDED JOINS** Another method involves simply butting the edges together. In order for them to fit together neatly, one edge of each of the four side sections has to be reduced slightly in size.

As before, cut out five equal-sized squares of clay. Put the base section on a bat.

Place one of the roller guides used when rolling out the slab so that its narrow edge is along one edge of a side section, and score along the side. Cut off the scored section with a craft knife.

5 Score and slip the upper edge of one side of the base section and the bottom edge of a side section. Fit the section into place on the base. Hold it for a second or two so the surfaces bond together. You will notice that the side panel does not fit the base exactly.

Score and slip the next edge of the base and the side of the section already in place, which is just short of the end of the base, plus the relevant inner and bottom edge of the next side section.

Butt the edges of the second section up against the first. Make sure that both sections sit squarely on the base. The first side will now be the correct size for the base. Continue until the box is completed.

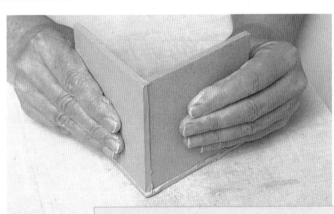

SEE ALSO
Basic skills: *Rolling slabs, pages 26–27*

SLABBED CANDLEHOLDER

In this project you will expand on the techniques you learned on pages 66–67 to construct slabs with a more difficult shape simply by adding a moulded slab to the top of the box shape. You will need a selection of stamps to create a design and a coloured slip for the surface finish, which will frame the pattern. Ask your supplier to recommend clay for Raku firing. If you do not have the right equipment, apply a simple glaze and fire in the conventional way.

Several coats of coloured slip were applied to the surface surrounding the stamp pattern. The surface was burnished to a high sheen before bisque firing to 960°C (1750°F).
The burnished area was first covered in a resist slip and then a Raku glaze. The piece was fired outside in a Raku kiln. Both slip and glaze were removed after firing, and the burnished surface polished with wax.

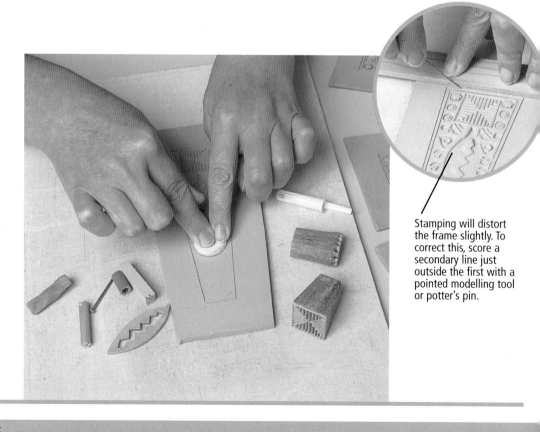

1 SIDE PANELS Roll out a large slab of clay and transfer it onto a board. Cut out a cardboard template: 10 cm (4 in.) along the base x 20 cm (8 in.) high, tapering to 6 cm (2½ in.) at the top. Use the template to cut out four panels from the slab.

Using a ruler or the roller guide, lightly score an inner frame to contain the stamp pattern. Use a selection of stamps to fill the framed area.

Stamping will distort the frame slightly. To correct this, score a secondary line just outside the first with a pointed modelling tool or potter's pin.

2 Join the panels together, scoring and slipping the edges and reinforcing the seams on the inside with thin coils of soft clay.

Neaten the edges on the outside with a kidney. Take care not to damage the stamped area as you work.

3 **MOULDING AND POSITIONING THE TOP** Cut a 13 cm (5 in.) square of clay from a freshly rolled slab. Place it inside or drape it over a round-bottomed plaster mould or kitchen bowl, with a cloth between the clay and the mould. Dry the clay to leather hard with a hair-dryer.

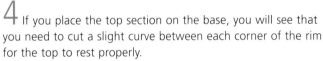

4 If you place the top section on the base, you will see that you need to cut a slight curve between each corner of the rim for the top to rest properly.

Use a curved surform to shave the excess clay a little at a time. Hold the base firmly with the other hand as you work.

5 Leave the top section in place on your mould so that you can fit the base to it. However, if the top was made inside the mould, it must be fitted to the base the correct way up.

Fit the sections together to measure the balance of top to bottom. When you are sure that the top is sitting squarely, mark the outline position lightly with a pin or pointed tool. Score and slip the marked area and the rim of the base and fit the sections together. Reinforce the join on the outside with a coil of soft clay, blending it in neatly.

SEE ALSO
Getting started: *Raku firing,* pages 20–21
Glaze recipes: pages 120–121
Decorating: *Stamps, page 34*

PROJECT 5: SLABBED CANDLEHOLDER 69

CONSTRUCTING WITH SOFT SLA

You can construct all kinds of creative projects by wrapping soft slabs around a simple mould, such as a cardboard tube, a glass or plastic bottle or any other cylindrical object. Once you have your basic cylindrical shape, you can manipulate and alter the form. You can use any type of clay to practise, but adding grog strengthens the clay, which will then hold its shape better.

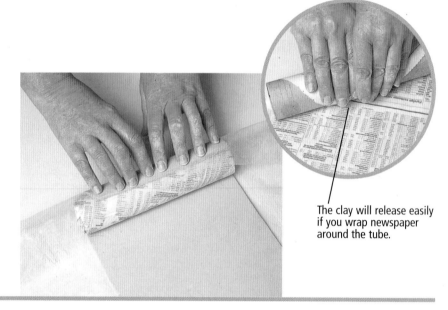

1 **FORMING** Roll out a 6-mm (¼-in.) thick slab of clay as shown on page 26. Cut a straight edge on one long side of the slab. When the clay is wrapped around the tube, the height of the slab should be slightly shorter than the tube. Do not worry if the opposite edge is uneven; it will form a feature.

Gently roll the clay around the tube. The plastic sheet will help hold the shape.

The clay will release easily if you wrap newspaper around the tube.

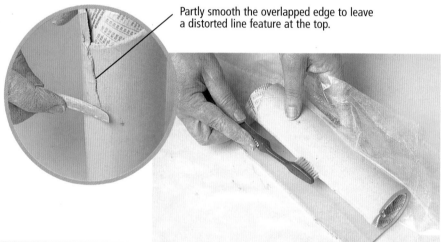

2 Where the clay overlaps, cut away the surplus to leave 6 mm (¼ in.) spare. Put the surplus slab to one side. Score and slip the edges, then join them together, making sure the clay fits neatly.

Smooth the overlapped clay together with a finger or wooden modelling tool. The distorted cut edge could become a feature of the pot, or you can smooth the area with a metal kidney.

Partly smooth the overlapped edge to leave a distorted line feature at the top.

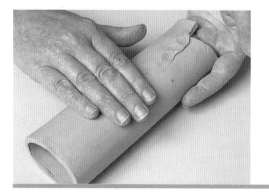

3 **CREATING THE VESSEL** Stand the cylinder upright, and dry the clay with a hair-dryer until it just holds its shape. Remove the tube and newspaper, and place the cylinder on its side. With one hand supporting the inside, gently ease the shape into an oval with the other hand.

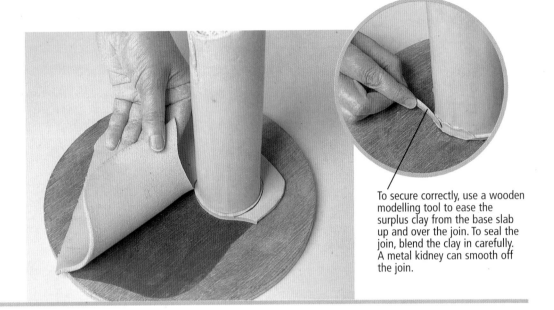

4 Place the surplus slab on a wooden bat. Position the oval vessel on top. Cut out the base so that it is slightly larger than the bottom rim of the vessel. Score and slip the base slab and rim. Secure the vessel in place.

To secure correctly, use a wooden modelling tool to ease the surplus clay from the base slab up and over the join. To seal the join, blend the clay in carefully. A metal kidney can smooth off the join.

Stamp a shell on the overlap detail to give it texture if desired.

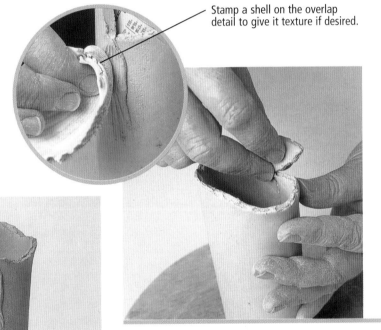

5 **FINISHING** To finish the vessel, rip the clay to enhance the detail where the slab was joined. If you prefer a neat finish, surform the edge level, and smooth it with a kidney.

6 The finished pot is ready for decoration or firing.

SEE ALSO
Basic skills: *Rolling slabs, page 26*

Decorating: *Creating textures, page 34*

SOFT SLABBED TEAPOT

In this project, you use the technique you have just learned for soft slabbing around a form, but on a slightly larger scale. You also learn how to cut and manipulate the clay to change the shape. All the components of the pot are made from soft slabs, except the handle. This is made from a flattened coil.

After bisque firing to 1000°C (1832°F) the pot was decorated with multiple glazes and wax resist patterning. It was fired to 1260°C (2300°F) in an electric kiln with a half-hour soak at the top temperature.

YOU WILL NEED

MATERIALS
Clay: finely grogged for hand building
Cylinder of at least 11.5 cm (4½ in.) diameter
Paper
Paintbrush

TOOLS
Roller guides
Hair-dryer
Rolling pin
Scalpel
Plastic or wooden rib tool
Hole-cutter

Carefully ease the edges together.

• Reinforce the inside with a coil of soft clay, and blend it in well.

1 **FORMING THE BODY** Roll out a slab of clay to fit around your cylinder. Use roller guides no thicker than 6 mm (¼ in.). Measure and cut the slab to 14 cm (5½ in.) width.

Make the cylinder, but only loosely join the edges. Firm the clay with a hair-dryer. Remove the form.

Using a paper template, cut out a V-shaped section that removes the original loose join. Score and slip the edges to be joined.

2 Fit the body of the pot onto a base slab. If you can get your hand inside the pot, reinforce the join further with a coil of soft clay.

Use a plastic or wooden rib tool to cut a small bevel around the base. Turn the pot over. Fit another slab to the top, securing it in the same way on the outside.

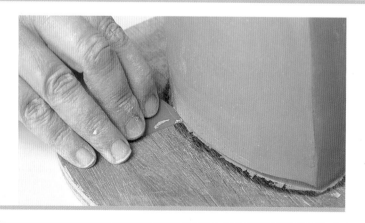

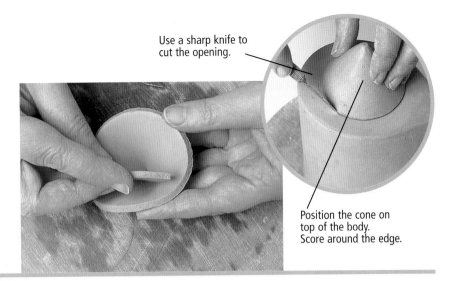

Use a sharp knife to cut the opening.

Position the cone on top of the body. Score around the edge.

3 MAKING THE LID Cut out a 7.5-cm (3-in.) diameter circle of clay from a slab scrap. Cut a line from the centre of the circle to the outer edge.

Manipulate the circle into a cone shape. Cut away the overlapped clay. Score and slip the edges, and join them together neatly.

4 Cut out another circle of clay 6 mm (¼ in.) wider than the circumference of the cone. Score and slip, then join both together neatly.

Cut out a ribbon of clay about 13 mm (½ in.) wide. Form it into a circle that will fit comfortably inside the opening. Fix the locating ring onto the underside of the lid. Hollow out the lid by cutting a circle within the locating ring.

Fix a tiny ball of clay on top of the lid. Pierce a small hole in the side of the cone.

Before the spout is fixed in place, a series of holes inside the area marked on the side of the pot can be made with a hole-cutter.

5 MAKING THE SPOUT Cover the thick handle of a paintbrush with paper and wrap a slab of clay around it. Firm the spout up a little with a hair-dryer.

Cut one end at approximately 45°. Experiment to get the correct angle of spout to body. Mark the position of the spout on the body, making sure that it is correctly aligned. Fix the spout in place, reinforcing it on the outside with a coil of soft clay.

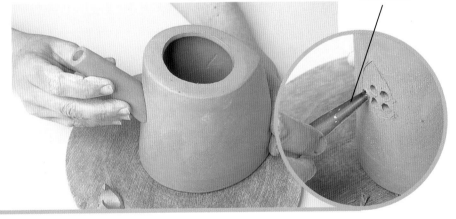

6 MAKING THE HANDLE Roll a thick coil of clay and flatten it as described on page 25. Cut the coil to approximately 25 mm (1 in.). Soften the edges with a finger. Using the edge of the roller guide, impress a ridge down the centre.

Hold one end of the coil on the top of the pot, and measure the length of the handle. Cut away any excess and fix the handle securely in place. Reinforce where necessary.

SEE ALSO
Basic skills: *Adapting rounded coils, page 25*
Decoration: *Wax resist, page 43*
Glaze recipes: *pages 120–121*

As discussed in Basic Skills (see pages 28–29) the technique of throwing requires endless amounts of practice. However, once mastered, it is extremely rewarding and allows you to produce many different wares quickly.

THROWING A BOWL

We can all make use of bowls in our homes, and they can be very satisfying shapes to throw, but some skill is required to get the visual balance of a good bowl right. This bowl is made using 1.8 kg (4 lb) of red earthenware clay. When thrown, the bowl measures approximately 15 cm (6 in.) deep and 25 cm (10 in.) wide when still wet.

Use both thumbs to make a preliminary indent in the clay before proceeding to opening the clay.

Start with the clay in a mushroom shape.

TIPS FOR SUCCESS
- Bowls can easily be knocked off centre by sudden hand movements. Move away from the clay gently and carefully.
- Do not allow water to accumulate inside the pot because the clay will become saturated and cause the pot to flop.
- Try to keep the inside curve of your bowl smooth to prevent the walls from collapsing.
- Keep the section of clay wall even at all times. One of the biggest problems for beginners is thinning out the clay at the base of a bowl too soon, so that the weight of clay above it cannot be supported.

1 **OPENING** Centre the clay. With the wheel turning swiftly, press the thumb of your right hand into the centre of the clay, while supporting the outer wall with the other hand. Press the thumb to within about 13 cm (½ in.) of the base, and then push the clay out sideways to widen the form. As the thumb moves towards the outer wall, raise it up a little to curve the inner floor.

Run your thumb over the base two or three times to consolidate the clay.

2 **LIFTING THE WALL** Position the thumb of your left hand at the outside base of the clay and your fingers over the rim and inside. Use your right hand as support by positioning it over the rim and left hand. Squeezing the thumb and fingers of your left hand together, slowly bring your hand up the side of the pot. Keep the heel of your right hand resting on the rim of the pot to consolidate the clay. The wheel should be turning faster than your hands are moving.

3 When throwing clay, it naturally wants to flare out into a bowl shape. It is very important not to allow this to happen at this stage. If it does, the form will not hold its shape when lifted further.

The first lift of the clay should be almost vertical to maintain control. It helps to leave the clay at the rim slightly thicker, so that there is enough clay to work with when the bowl is widened.

4 Lubricate the pot. With your arms held tight to your body and your right forearm resting on the edge of the wheel tray, support the inner wall and rim of the pot with the fingers of your left hand.

With the fingers of the right hand, make a groove into the clay wall at the base of the pot, where the clay meets the wheel head. Position the thumb and fingers of your left hand over the rim, immediately above the groove, and squeeze them together; this will create a bulge.

Place the knuckle of your right hand under the bulge on the outside of the bowl, and then begin to force the bulge upwards, with the knuckle pressing against the fingers of the left hand on the inside.

• As you raise the bulge, keep your elbow tucked into your body to steady your hands.

As the knuckle approaches the rim of the pot, slowly relax the pressure so that the rim is not thinned too much.

5 As the bulge reaches the top of the bowl, gently squeeze and smooth the clay to consolidate the rim. Repeat the lifting process, following the same method. Remember to lubricate the surface from time to time. Sponge out any excess water inside the bowl.

Before you begin to swell the body of the bowl, remove any excess clay from the wheel head with a throwing rib. Create a bevel under the base of the pot by removing a sliver of clay with the throwing rib. This helps to wire the bowl off the wheel head when it is finished.

6 **SHAPING** The final shape of the bowl is formed using the throwing rib. Starting just above the bevel at the base of the bowl, use the rib on the outside wall, supported on the inside by the fingers of the left hand. Push the clay against the rib to smooth and shape the wall as they travel up the bowl, all the way to the rim.

The finishing of the bowl should be carried out with the wheel turning fairly slowly. Sponge out any water from inside the bowl.

To remove the bowl, flood the wheel head with water. Keeping your cutting wire taut and completely flat to the wheel, pull it towards your body under the base of the bowl. With dry hands around the base, slide the bowl across the wheel and lift it onto a dry board.

7 **TURNING THE FOOT RING** When your bowl has dried to the leather-hard stage, turn it over and centre it onto the wheel head. Turn the base to form a foot ring that is in proportion to the rest of the bowl. This can be tricky, and also depends on the amount of clay left behind from the throwing process. Turning is a very satisfying process, which can be overdone so check the thickness of the clay wall regularly to avoid turning straight through it!

SEE ALSO
Basic skills: *Centring clay, page 28; Turning, pages 30–31*

THROWING A PLATE

To make a flat plate with an even base takes quite a lot of practice because the hand movements used are very different from those used for taller forms. However, plates provide wonderful surfaces to decorate, so it is well worth taking the time to learn to throw them well.

This plate is made from 1.6 kg (3½ lb) of clay and measures approximately 28 cm (11 in.) wide when still wet. You can use any smooth clay that is recommended for throwing.

1 **OPENING** With a bat firmly fixed to the wheel head, centre the lump of clay. With the wheel turning swiftly, support the clay on the outside with the left hand, without applying any pressure, and then press down with the heel of the right hand to create a depression in the centre of the clay. Keeping the right elbow high to apply downwards pressure, push the clay outwards across the bat. Remember to lubricate from time to time.

THROWING ON A BAT

Plates are usually thrown on wooden bats because they are difficult to remove from the wheel head while still wet. Fixing a bat to the wheel head is similar to throwing a plate. Follow the first two steps, but at stage two, continue to force the clay towards the edge of the wheel head until the clay is completely flat.

Smooth the base flat with your fingers or a throwing rib, and then press a finger down into the flat clay close to the centre to create an indented ring. Make a series of concentric rings out to the edge of the clay disk.

Place your bat on top of the clay, making sure that it is centred. Give the bat a firm thump in the centre with a clenched fist. If it moves, give it another thump until it holds in place.

2 Using the side of the right hand, continue to push the clay out towards the side of the bat while supporting the side with the left hand. Do not worry about the small hill of clay in the centre of the base of the plate at this stage; it will be incorporated into the plate at a later stage.

Push the right hand down on the left hand to add extra pressure.

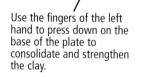

Use the fingers of the left hand to press down on the base of the plate to consolidate and strengthen the clay.

3 Use the side of your right hand to press the hill in the centre of the plate flat, and then move the hand slowly outwards away from the centre. Repeat several times.

To consolidate the clay in the base, place the right hand on top of the left and exert downwards pressure on the fingers. Continue to apply pressure from the centre to the edge.

Now place the thumb of the left hand on the outside of the ridge of clay, which has been left around the edge. The fingers of the left hand should be positioned on the inside, with the right hand resting on the ridge and over the left hand. Gently squeeze the thumb and fingers of the left hand together, while gently pressing down with the right hand to consolidate the clay on the rim.

4 **FORMING THE RIM** Position the thumb of your left hand under the rim, with the fingers on the inside and the right hand over the left to keep it steady. Squeezing gently between the fingers and thumb, very gradually draw the clay outwards and slightly upwards with the wheel rotating slightly more slowly. It is important to be aware of your hand movements at this stage because, if your hands move too fast, the rim can become uneven.

Place both hands on the rib to exert downwards pressure and keep the pressure even.

• Keep the pressure going right across the plate to the rim.

5 Before you finish off the rim completely, use a throwing rib to smooth the base of the plate for the last time. Starting from the centre and applying gentle pressure, move the rib across the base to the outer rim. This compresses the clay in the base and removes any irregularities left behind. Any excess water that is moved outwards can be sponged away at the rim.

Plates should be wired while still in place on the bat and wheel head.

• Hold the wire taut between your hands, with the forefingers pressing it flat on the surface of the bat.

The wire should be drawn from back to front.

6 Use the rib to create a bevel at the base of the pot as a guide for the cutting wire. Position the rib flat on the bat, and then push it slightly into the outer base to remove a sliver of clay.

Support the underside of the rim with the left hand, and then very carefully use the rib to lower the rim to its final shape. Use only very light pressure.

Wire the plate underneath. Carefully remove the bat from the wheel head with the plate still on it. When the plate is dry enough not to distort when handled, wire it again and transfer it to a dry bat.

7 TURNING Once the clay is stiff, but still damp, it can be turned. Fix another bat to the wheel head as before. Dampen the surface of the bat and the rim of the plate, and centre it upside down. Hold your little finger against the rim of the plate and rotate the wheel. The gap between the rim and the finger should remain constant. If it does not, reposition the plate and start again.

Hold a ribbon tool in the right hand and rest the left hand on the plate with the thumb on the tool. With the wheel turning fairly swiftly, work the tool from the centre outwards to remove a thin layer of clay from the base.

8 Remove the excess clay, which was supporting the rim, with a curved edge ribbon tool. Try to form a nice curve, working from the foot to the rim, and removing the clay gradually. Obviously, you will need to remove more clay where it is thickest or uneven.

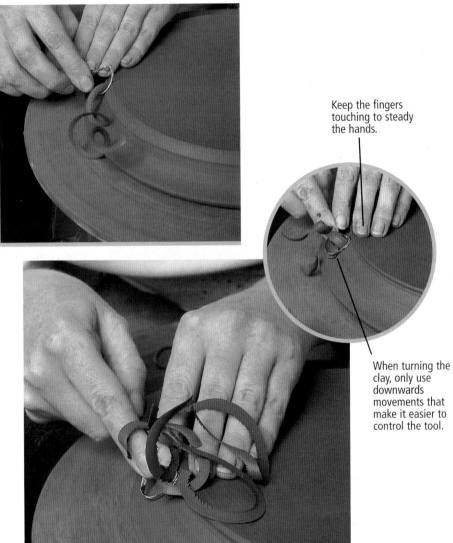

Keep the fingers touching to steady the hands.

When turning the clay, only use downwards movements that make it easier to control the tool.

9 **TURNING A ROLL FOOT** Using the ribbon tool, slightly undercut the base at the outer edge. Round off the edge so that it cuts into the rim slightly further down, to form what looks like a tiny secondary rim. You will now be able to glaze up to the ridge, which forms a platform. The middle of the plate should dip slightly so that, ideally, only the outside edge sits on the surface when the plate is fired. To achieve this, remove a little clay from the centre of the plate, reducing the amount as you work outwards and stopping just before the edge.

10 Carefully lift the plate off the bat. Sponge the edges to remove any marks and smooth the clay.

Allow the plate to dry out thoroughly before bisque firing.

SEE ALSO
Basic skills: *Centring, page 28*
Turning, pages 30–31

THROWN CHEESE BELL

This project incorporates the techniques of throwing a plate and a bowl from the previous pages. You will learn how to measure your pots to fit together and how to add details such as knobs.

Red earthenware clay has been used here to form a base for majolica glaze decoration later, but you could use any clay recommended for throwing. The choice of clay is most relevant to the type of surface decoration you intend to use.

After bisque firing to 1000°C (1832°F) various areas of the bell were wax resisted to form contrasting details. The plate and dome were covered in a white tin glaze. Underglaze motifs were then sponged onto the surface. The bell was fired to 1080°C (1976°F) in an electric kiln.

YOU WILL NEED
MATERIALS
Red earthenware clay

FOR DECORATION
Majolica glaze
Underglaze colours

TOOLS
Callipers
Wheel
Ribbon tool
Craft knife
Sponge
Hole-making tool

1 USING CALLIPERS Measure the inside dimension of the plate (see pages 76–79). Make sure the callipers are tight so that they will not move after measuring. This will also be the measurement for the width of the dome cover.

2 From 1.4 kg (3 lb) of clay, throw a bowl up to step five of Throwing a bowl (see pages 74–75). Check the width of the rim regularly – it should match the measurement of the callipers.

Leave enough clay at the rim to form the base of the dome. Use the sharp end of the rib to create a groove in the wall just below the rim, pushing from the inside with the left fingers and supporting the rim with the left thumb. Slightly flatten the rim on top so that it will sit more comfortably on the plate. Check the size again with the callipers. If the bowl is not wide enough, ease it out just a little more.

The rim of the bell is kept slightly thicker for extra strength.

The wall of the bell should remain relatively straight as it is lifted.

• Very little shaping is done at this stage because the dome will be turned when the clay has dried to leather hard.

3 **TURNING** Allow the bowl dome to dry to the leather-hard stage. Dampen the wheel head and the rim of the bowl and then centre it, using the concentric rings on the wheel head as a guide.

Using a ribbon tool, begin to form the outer curve of the dome. The wheel should be moving quite quickly as you hold your left hand on the dome, with the thumb resting on the tool to hold it steady. You will find that there is quite a lot of clay to remove.

4 Continue turning with the ribbon tool until a smooth, rounded curve is formed on the dome. Check the thickness of the walls from time to time by removing the dome from the wheel and then re-centring it. This may feel like a hassle, but until you can gauge the thickness automatically it is a wise precaution to take.

5 **THROWING THE KNOB** Using a craft knife, cross-hatch an area in the middle of the top of the dome where the knob will be positioned. Form a little knob of clay in the hands, dampen it, and then press it down onto the cross-hatched area. Centre the ball of clay using a small amount of water for lubrication, and then form the shape into a knob.

6 Press the little finger into the base of the knob to form an undercut; this makes the dome easy to grip when in use. Remove any excess water or slurry from around the knob with a sponge.

Carefully remove the dome from the wheel head, and leave it to dry again. Use a hole-making tool to hollow out the knob from the inside.

7 Check that the finished dome fits the plate, and allow them to dry together. You can bisque fire the dome or bell in place on the plate, but they must be fired separately when glazed.

SEE ALSO
Getting started: *Kilns, pages 18–21*
Basic skills: *Throwing, pages 28–31*
Decorating: *Wax resist and Majolica, pages 43 and 45*
Glaze recipes: *pages 120–121*

THROWING A BASIC CYLINDER

The cylinder is the basis for most upright forms, such as jugs and vases, and as such is an essential skill of throwing. As with all skills, you will only improve with practice.

A good way of measuring your progress is to throw the same weight of clay each time so that differences in height and shape will be obvious. There are no real rules for any type of pottery making – the potter must find success through his or her own discoveries and mistakes. If you achieve results through methods you have developed yourself, that is perfectly valid and you are more likely to remember the process. There are, however, some basic principles that will help you on your way.

Using the thumbs press the clay down firmly at the base of the pot.

1 **OPENING** Centre a ball of well-prepared clay. With the hands locked in a strong position, cup the hands around the clay and press the thumb of the right hand directly down through the centre to within about 6 mm (¼ in.) of the wheel head. The wheel should be turning swiftly. Remember to lubricate the clay from time to time. Continue to cup the clay with your hands as you use the thumb to open and widen the hole. Keep your thumb at a fixed level as you move it outwards to form a flat, smooth base. Run your fingers over the base from the centre outwards several times to consolidate the clay.

• This consolidates the clay and makes the base stronger, which prevents S-shaped cracks from appearing later.

2 **LIFTING THE WALL** Lift the clay wall by placing the thumb of the left hand at the base of the pot on the outside. Push the thumb in slightly to create a small hollow. Curl the rest of the left hand over the rim of the pot to the inside, and rest the right hand on the rim and over the left hand for extra support.

Squeeze the finger and thumb of the left hand together as the clay wall is lifted, maintaining the pressure until you get almost to the top. Consolidate the clay on the rim by continuing to rest the right hand on it gently as the wall rises.

3 As the cylinder rises, push it in slightly to narrow the form, maintaining the position of the right hand on the rim. Try to keep the walls an even thickness during the whole lifting process, but leave the rim a little thicker until the end. With practice, this stage of the lifting process will only need to be done once.

Keep both hands in contact with one another. This helps to steady the hands.

4 KNUCKLING UP With your left fingers still inside the pot, push out a slight bulge at the base. Place the knuckle of the right hand under the bulge on the outside. Gently push the bulge up the wall of the pot with the knuckle. Your fingers on the inside should continue to push out the bulge as the knuckle rises just below them. This whole process should be done in one continuous action from base to rim.

Use the web of skin between the thumb and first finger to smooth the rim of the pot.

5 Repeat the knuckle lift two or three times more until the cylinder has reached its full height.

Leave the rim of the pot slightly thicker than the walls for a neat finish. This small detail gives the cylinder visual lift, often making the difference between a form that looks finished and one that does not.

6 While supporting the wall on the inside with the fingers of the left hand and on the outside with the thumb, use the index finger of the right hand to smooth the rim. Apply only a small amount of pressure.

7 SMOOTHING OFF To remove the throwing rings for a smoother decorating surface first cut a bevel at the base of the pot with the pointed end of the rib. With your left hand inside the pot and the rib in your right hand against the cylinder wall, use your fingers to push the clay against the rib as it rises up. Make sure the rib and fingers travel slowly and evenly up the wall to just below the rim. Remember to leave the clay slightly thicker at the top. Do not use water. The aim of this is to remove excess water and compact the clay.

To remove the cylinder, hold the wire taut and flat to the wheel head while drawing it towards your body. Carefully lift the pot onto a dry board.

Cylinder bases should not need to be trimmed.

SEE ALSO
Basic skills: *Centring, page 28*

A THROWN JUG

Throwing a jug is a natural step on from the basic cylinder and requires only a few modifications. In this project you will learn how to adapt your cylinder and how to add a pulled handle. You can use any clay suitable for throwing. Here, red earthenware clay has been used as a base for slip decoration and sgraffito.

The jug has been decorated with coloured slips and paper resist with sgraffito detail. A simple earthenware transparent glaze was poured over the jug before firing to 1080°C (1976°F) in an electric kiln.

YOU WILL NEED

MATERIALS
Red earthenware clay

FOR DECORATION
Coloured slips
Transparent glaze

TOOLS
Wheel
Ribbon tool
Craft knife
Sponge
Brushes
Potter's pin

1 Throw a basic cylinder shape following the technique on pages 82–83. Use a sponge to wipe out excess water from the inside. Cut a bevel at the base of the cylinder with the pointed end of the throwing rib. Smooth off the wall with the side of the rib to remove the throwing rings.

While the cylinder for the jug is still in position on the wheel head, sponge around the rim to remove excess water and smooth off.

2 **FORMING THE LIP** With the cylinder still in place on the wheel, but no longer rotating, use the thumb and first finger of the right hand to gently smooth an area of the rim flat. Carefully pull the clay upwards as you thin it to extend the height a little. Do not overthin the clay, or the spout will look sharp and unrefined.

The wheel should be rotating fairly slowly for sponging off.

Only use one hand for this job because the other hand will snag the clay as the lubrication is removed.

3 **SHAPING THE LIP** Place the finger and thumb of the left hand on either side of the flattened area and gently squeeze them in slightly. Using the first finger of your right hand, carefully shape the pouring lip. Your finger should be well lubricated as you move it from side to side, gently easing the clay downwards and curving the lip over slightly.

Using both hands, lift the jug carefully off the wheel head onto a dry bat.

Flood the wheel head with water before wiring underneath the jug.

• To avoid leaving slurry marks on the surface, clean excess clay off your hands before lifting the jug off the wheel.

4 Flood the wheel head with water, then carefully wire under the base of the jug, keeping the wire taut and flat. Lift the jug off the wheel onto a dry board. Allow the jug to dry to the leather-hard stage.

5 **PULLING THE HANDLE** To make the handle for your jug, form a fat coil of clay and hold it in your left hand. Lubricate your right hand and the clay with water, then stroke it until it is smooth and lengthened a little.

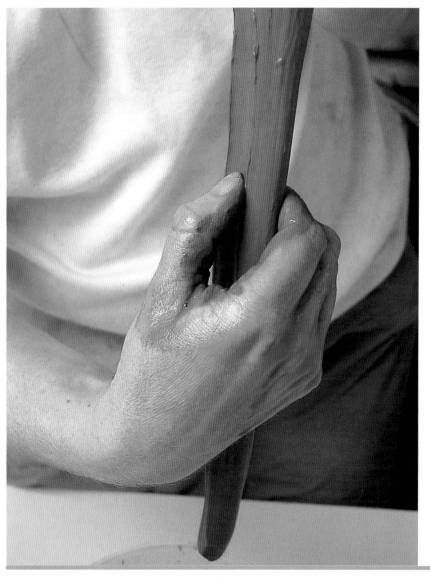

6 Place the thumb of the right hand over the front of the coil of clay, and wrap the fingers around the back to form a bend. Gently run the hand down the length of the coil, maintaining this position. As you gently ease the clay downwards it should lengthen and thin out. After a few strokes, rotate the coil so that the profile is maintained and your fingers do not thin one area more than another.

Continue to stroke and pull the handle until the required length and size is achieved. Place the handle flat on a board, or along the edge of the work table, so that it hangs over the edge.

7 **JOINING** Cross-hatch the area on the outside wall of the jug at the spot where you will attach the top of the handle; this should be directly opposite the pouring lip.

Dab a little slurry onto the prepared area on the jug, press the thicker end of the handle into place, then smooth the join onto the jug with your fingers.

When adding handles, it is important to blend the clay neatly and thoroughly onto the wall of the vessel.

• The size of the handle should be proportionate to the size of the jug.

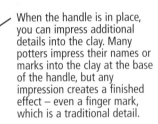

When the handle is in place, you can impress additional details into the clay. Many potters impress their names or marks into the clay at the base of the handle, but any impression creates a finished effect – even a finger mark, which is a traditional detail.

8 Curve the handle into a loop, judging the size by eye. Mark the position of the end of the handle on the wall of the jug, and cross-hatch the area as before. Affix the handle with a little slurry, and smooth it with a finger. Allow the handle to firm up.

The jug is now complete and ready for decoration with coloured slips, paper resist and sgraffito.

SEE ALSO
Decorating: *Slip decoration, pages 37–41; Sgraffito, page 39*

Glaze recipes: *pages 120–121*

MAKING A PRESS MOULD

Most people think that making plaster moulds is difficult and that they will need extra equipment and materials. However, provided you follow a few simple rules and are meticulous in your preparation, this is not really the case.

This technique shows you how to make a press mould from an everyday kitchen item – in this case, a stainless steel bowl. A plastic or wooden bowl would work equally well. When choosing a model for your mould, it is important that the shape doesn't have ridges or raised areas; these will create undercuts, which prevent the model from being released from the mould.

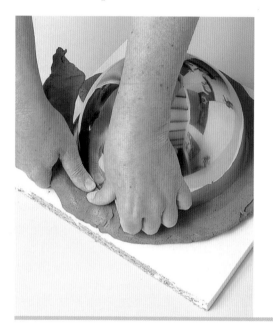

1 Because the base of the chosen kitchen bowl has a lip, which would cause undercutting, the model has to be secured to a nonabsorbent board with a thick coil of clay.

Once the model has been secured to the board, flatten the coil with a scraping tool, making sure not to leave any clay on the model. It will help if you can get the clay as level as possible because this will be the rim of the mould when it has been cast. Aim to make this clay base about 25 mm (1 in.) wide around the bowl.

2 **SOFT SOAPING** This is a wise precaution if you are at all concerned about how easily the model will release from the mould. Paint a layer of watered-down mould maker's size or soft soap onto the model with a soft brush, taking care not to disturb the clay base. Gently wipe the soap off again with a barely damp sponge, and then repeat the process twice more.

TIPS FOR SUCCESS
- Plaster contaminates clay and, if accidentally trapped in clay bodies, will cause explosions during firing. If possible, avoid working with plaster in your workshop. If this is not possible, work on plastic sheeting and have plenty of newspapers on hand to mop up spills, along with a bag-lined dustbin for quick disposal of surplus plaster. Always clean up thoroughly before working with clay again.
- NEVER wash excess plaster down the sink. It will set in the pipe and cause a blockage that will be impossible to remove.
- Wipe excess plaster from gloves or hands with newspaper before washing them.
- Use newspaper to clean out your plaster bucket after use, and then immediately transfer the newspaper to a bag-lined dustbin.

3 **MAKING A COTTLE** You can use scraps of linoleum, or cushion-type floor covering, to form a cottle, or wall, around the model. Alternatively, use a thick slab of clay, but remember that you will not be able to reuse it because it will be contaminated. It is vital to secure the cottle in place.

Here, the linoleum cottle has been wrapped around the model twice and secured with tape. To prevent plaster from seeping out of the bottom, seal the base of the cottle with a coil of soft clay.

4 Estimate the amount of plaster/water you will need to cover your model, and allow for at least 25 mm (1 in.) extra at the top. (This will be the base of the mould when it is turned over.) It can be difficult to estimate amounts when you start to mould, so aim to make more rather than less. Dispose of the surplus in the bin, or have some sprig moulds ready to cast (see page 94) to avoid too much waste.

Mix the plaster, and carefully pour it over the model.

5 When all the plaster has covered the model, agitate the surface gently with the palm of the hand for a second or two to release any trapped air bubbles. With the tip of your finger, burst any bubbles that rise to the surface. Leave the mould to set until the heating process is over.

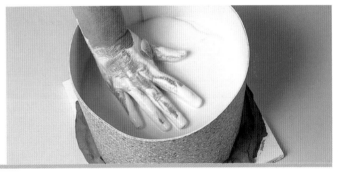

6 **REMOVING THE EDGES** Carefully remove the cottle from around the mould.

Lift the model out of the mould; this should be quite easy if you soft soaped it well enough. Use a surform blade to slightly round off all the sharp outer edges on the mould. Put the mould somewhere warm to dry out. The top of the kiln is perfect, but raise the mould on props to allow air to circulate around it.

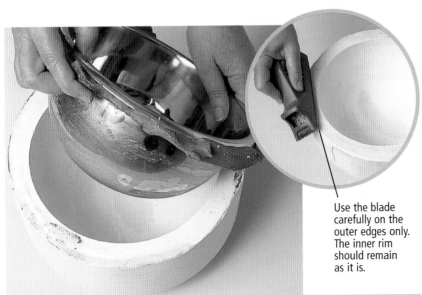

Use the blade carefully on the outer edges only. The inner rim should remain as it is.

SEE ALSO
Basic skills: *Mixing plaster for mould making, page 32*

PROJECT 9

MOULDED BOWL
WITH FLATTENED COIL EXTENSION

Moulds are wonderfully versatile and can be used to make complete clay forms, or as a starting point or base from which a form can be built up. Many potters use them in this way because so many different forms can be created and replicated as necessary. This project demonstrates how to use and build onto the basic bowl-shaped mould made on pages 88–89. You can use any clay for this project.

A wax resist pattern was painted directly onto the bisque-fired bowl before a turquoise Raku glaze was applied. The bowl was fired in a Raku kiln, followed by a post-firing reduction in a sawdust-filled metal bin with a tight-fitting lid.

YOU WILL NEED
MATERIALS
Clay
Mould
Plastic sheet

FOR DECORATION
White decorating slip

TOOLS
Craft knife
Sponge
Metal kidney
Rubber kidney
Roller guides
Hair-dryer
Wooden bat
Toothbrush
Surform blade

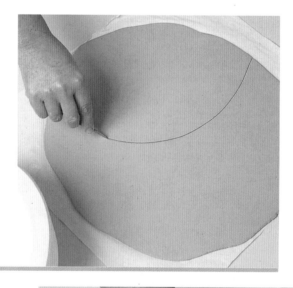

1 **CUTTING** Roll out a large slab of clay no thicker than 6 mm (¼ in.). The amount required depends on the size of your mould, but you will probably need more than you think because of the way the clay is cut to fit into the mould.

Use a craft knife to cut out two large semicircles of clay. Each semicircle should fit approximately half of the mould, with about 25 mm (1 in.) overlap in the middle.

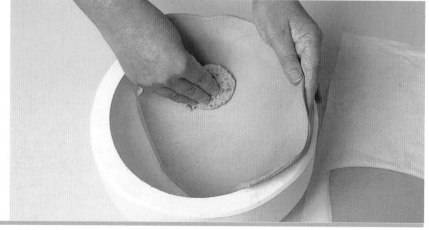

2 Carefully lift the first section of clay off the plastic sheet, and place it into the mould. Be careful not to crease it. Ease the clay into place using a barely damp sponge to avoid trapping air.

When the first section is in place, position the second section in the mould in the same way, allowing about 25 mm (1 in.) overlap in the middle.

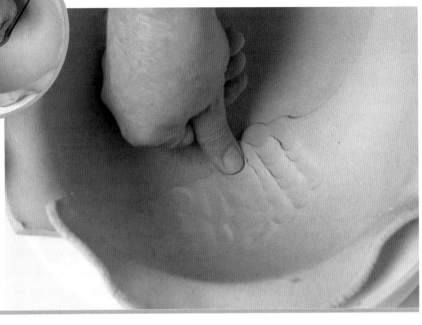

Turn the mould carefully with one hand as you smooth the surface.

Smooth the interior of the bowl with a rubber kidney to help compact the clay over the join and prepare the surface for later decoration.

Do not remove surplus clay around the rim until the interior is finished.

3 Using a thumb or finger, blend the two sections of clay together thoroughly. Work from side to side of the overlapped sections to force out any air that may be trapped between the layers. When the sections are blended together, remove any surplus clay with a metal kidney, then smooth over the surface with a rubber kidney.

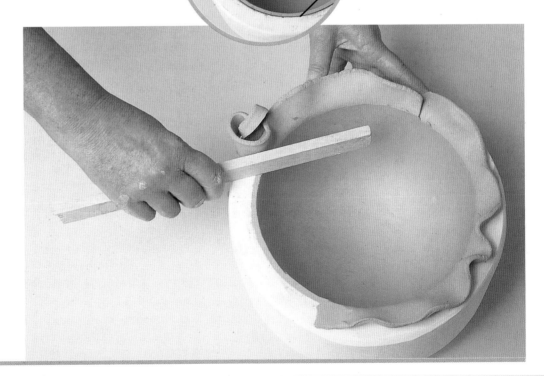

The mould should be rotated on a turntable, or banding wheel, to ensure that the clay dries evenly.

A hair-dryer is one of the most useful tools for the potter; it allows you to quickly dry clay, readying it for the next stage.

The clay is sufficiently dried when it begins to shrink away from the edge of the mould.

4 Use one of the roller guides to remove the surplus clay at the rim of the bowl. Position the guide flat on the rim of the mould, and draw the clay towards your body. Remove the excess in small sections to avoid dragging the clay out of the mould. Always use a wooden tool for this task to avoid scratching the mould and contaminating the clay with plaster.

When the rim is level, set the mould aside while the clay firms up and starts to shrink away from the sides of the mould.

5 Place a wooden bat over the mould, and then turn both over to release the bowl.

Roll a thin coil of soft clay. Carefully ease it into the join on the outside of the bowl. Press it gently into place with a finger, then remove any excess with a metal kidney or scraper. Smooth over the join with a rubber kidney to finish off. When you have finished you should not be able to see any evidence of the join.

Make sure the bowl is level on the coil before finishing off the rim.

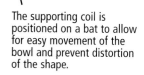

Support the bowl on a coil of soft clay to finish the rim off neatly.

The supporting coil is positioned on a bat to allow for easy movement of the bowl and prevent distortion of the shape.

6 **FLATTENED COIL EXTENSION** Roll out a thick coil of clay and form it into a ring on which to sit your bowl temporarily.

Roll out another thick coil of clay that is long enough to fit around the rim of the bowl. Flatten it straight. Score and slip the rim of the bowl using a toothbrush and water. Fit the coil into place so that the wall of the bowl is extended by about 50 mm (2 in.).

Neaten the rim, using a scraping tool or rubber kidney to carefully round the edge.

Support the wall of the bowl with one hand as you work around the rim.

Sit the bowl on a bat and rotate it on a turntable to avoid distorting the shape as you neaten the rim.

7 Reinforce the join between the bowl and the coil, both inside and out, with a thin coil of soft clay. Blend the soft coils in well. Remove any excess with a metal kidney. You may need to refine the extended coil by scraping away a little more clay to make it the same thickness as the wall of the moulded section.

Level off the rim of the bowl with a surform blade. It helps if you can do this with the bowl elevated at eye level. Finally, slightly round off the rim with a rubber kidney to soften the shape visually.

8 Turn the bowl upside down again onto a bat and remove the temporary supporting coil. Roll out another coil of clay to form the foot ring. The thickness of this coil should relate directly to the size of your bowl and it should be thick enough to support the bowl's visual weight.

Form the coil into a ring, making sure the join is secure. Rest the ring on the underside of the bowl, and mark the position with a wooden tool. Score and slip the marked area on the bowl and the underside of the ring, and then fit it into place.

Reinforce the ring inside and outside with some tiny coils of soft clay. Allow the foot ring to firm up a little before turning the bowl the right way up.

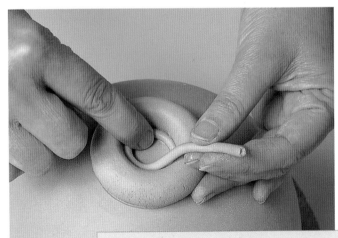

SEE ALSO
Getting started: *Raku firing, pages 20–21*

Basic skills: *Rolling coils, page 24; Rolling slabs, page 26*

MAKING A DRAPED SLAB
AND SPRIG MOULD

Most of us can find an everyday kitchen item from which to make a mould, but if you do not have anything suitable, try a car boot sale or a secondhand shop. The model for this mould is not very inspiring in its metal form; the shape is transformed when made in clay. Look for a model that is not too deep, with an open form to allow for easy casting in plaster.

When plaster casting, it is always useful to have some way of using up the surplus if you have overestimated the amount required. By preparing a model for a sprig mould in advance, you have the perfect solution to the problem. Sprigs can be very useful for surface decoration of bowls and vessels, or even tiles, where they give low-relief detail. The sprigs made here will be used later to form part of the detail in the tile project on page 102.

1 **RESIST LAYER** Prepare your model for plaster casting by applying a resist layer of soft soap (mould maker's size) to the surface with a paintbrush (see Making a press mould, page 88).

TIP
To avoid vastly overestimating the quantity, measure the amount of water your model will hold, then weigh out the equivalent amount of plaster. You will still have some excess because the plaster adds bulk, so this is where sprig moulds come in handy.

2 **SPRIG MOULDS** To make your sprig mould, you will need a tile or a piece of nonabsorbent board such as Formica. Decide on simple shapes for the sprigs, and cut them out as cardboard templates. (Here, Perspex templates of a leaf and flower have been used). Roll out a small, thin slab of clay about 3 mm (1/8 in.) thick and place it on the tile. Position the templates over the clay, and cut out the shapes using a sharp, pointed craft knife. Remove all excess clay from around the shapes.

3 When making any type of mould, it is important to avoid undercuts. These are areas on the model that would trap plaster when cast, making it impossible for the clay to release from the mould. Round off the edges of your sprig models so that they have a slight bevel from the upper surface down to the base. Use a modelling tool with a fine point for this job, and take the time to get it right.

Once you are sure that there are no undercuts in the sprig models, you can add some surface detail if you wish.

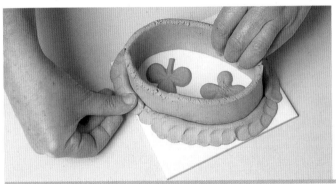

4 Roll a thick coil of clay and flatten it. Position the coil around the sprig models so that it forms a wall to contain the plaster. Allow at least 13 mm (½ in.) distance from the edges of the sprigs. Reinforce the wall with a coil of soft clay.

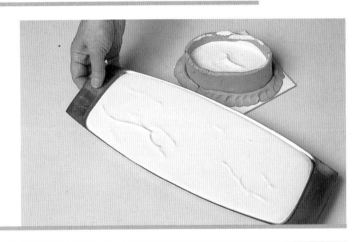

5 CASTING THE MODEL Prepare an appropriate quantity of plaster for the size of your model.

Pour the plaster into the prepared model until it is level with the top. Cast the sprig mould with the surplus. Very gently lift the model containing the plaster a fraction off the work surface, and tap it back down to bring any air bubbles to the surface. Leave both moulds to one side for the plaster to set.

6 THE FOOT When the plaster has just set in the draped slab mould model, use a sharp tool to mark out an area on the base roughly 25 mm (1 in.) in from the outer edge. Score the inner section of the marked area, using a cross-hatch action. This will form a key for the plaster foot.

Roll another thick coil of clay. Flatten it as before to form a wall for the foot. Position the coil around the scored area, and reinforce it with another coil of soft clay.

SEE ALSO
Basic skills: *Rolling coils, pages 24–25; Mixing plaster for mould making, page 32*

7 Prepare another quantity of plaster sufficient to form a foot on your model about 38–50 mm (1½–2 in.) deep. Pour the plaster into the foot model, and again give it a little tap to bring any air bubbles to the surface. Put the mould to one side to allow the plaster foot to set.

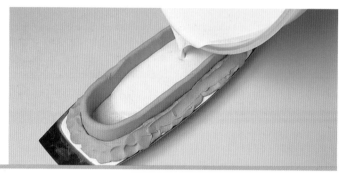

8 Lift the sprig mould off the tile carefully. Using a surform blade, carefully shave the edges to round them off. Remove any jagged bits that could break off later and contaminate your clay. To remove the clay sprigs, press a small ball of soft clay onto the back, and then lift the sprig out. Dispose of these sprigs, as they could be contaminated with plaster. Put the mould somewhere warm to dry out thoroughly.

Carefully remove the draped slab mould from the model, and surform all edges in the same way to round them off.

9 **DRAWING THE DESIGN** Place the draped slab model on a piece of tracing paper. Draw around the base with a pencil. Cut out the base shape, and draw a pattern of your choice inside the outline. Turn the tracing paper over. Place it over the mould so that it covers what will be the base of the dish when made in clay. Transfer the design onto the plaster by drawing over the pattern lines. Very carefully, using one hand to steady the other, score the design into the plaster with a modelling tool. A wooden tool should do the job well at this stage because the plaster is still quite soft.

Use a soft brush to remove any plaster on the surface as you work, and dispose of it carefully.

10 If you do not want to score a design into the bottom of the dish, you could cut out a template of the base from blown vinyl wallpaper. This allows you to change the relief pattern in the base of the dish more freely. Fix the paper temporarily to the plaster with some double-sided tape.

The finished moulds, ready for use.

HORS D'OEUVRES DISH

This project shows you how to use the draped slab mould from pages 94–96. You will also learn how to make handles from the relief detail carved into the mould. Details like these give the form visual continuity and a much more finished look.

You can use any smooth clay, although a white clay would be best. This is because the glaze finish needs to break over the relief pattern in the base of the dish and bright glaze colours work best over white clays.

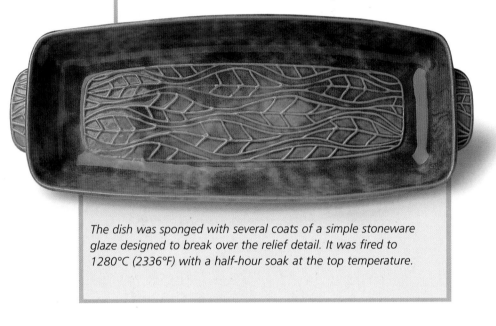

The dish was sponged with several coats of a simple stoneware glaze designed to break over the relief detail. It was fired to 1280°C (2336°F) with a half-hour soak at the top temperature.

YOU WILL NEED

MATERIALS
Smooth white clay
Draped slab mould
Plastic sheet

FOR DECORATION
Glazes

TOOLS
Sponge
Rolling pin
Metal kidney
Rubber kidney
Banding wheel
Roller guide
Toothbrush

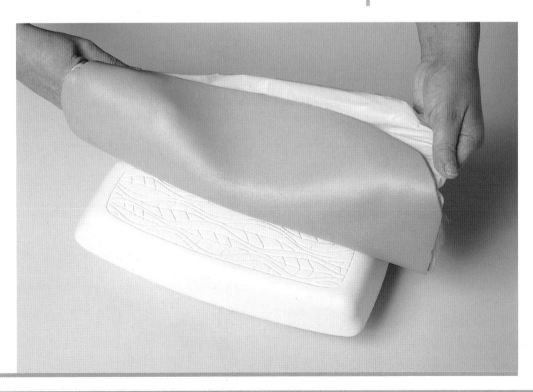

1 **COVERING THE MOULD** Roll out a slab of clay on a plastic sheet. It should be no thicker than 6 mm (¼ in.) and large enough to fit over the entire mould. Carefully lift them together and cover the mould with the slab.

When the slab is correctly placed, remove the sheet.

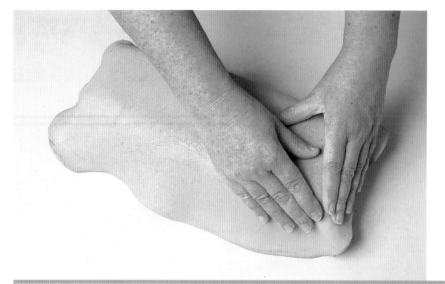

2 Using both hands, gently ease the clay over the edges of the mould. Try to avoid creasing or overlapping the clay, and do not press so hard that you make finger marks. Use a barely damp sponge if it is easier.

Before removing the surplus from the underside, smooth the surface of the clay with a metal kidney to ensure a good fit to the mould.

3 Gently roll over the clay on the mould with a rolling pin to ensure that the relief pattern is taken up in the base. Do not roll too hard because you will distort the clay. One light roll sideways and one lengthways should be enough.

Smooth over the dish with a rubber kidney to remove any possible irregularities on the surface.

Position the mould on a turntable for ease of movement.

• The left hand rotates the mould from the underside to avoid leaving finger marks in the clay as the surface is smoothed.

4 Lift the mould onto a banding wheel. Using a roller guide, carefully remove the overlapping clay. Hold the end of the guide level with the underside of the mould, and push it from front to back as you work sideways in small movements.

Removing the excess in this way helps avoid dragging the clay away from the plaster and distorting the shape of the dish.

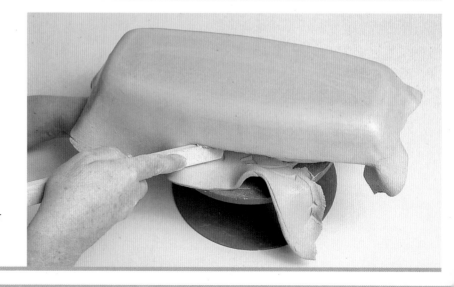

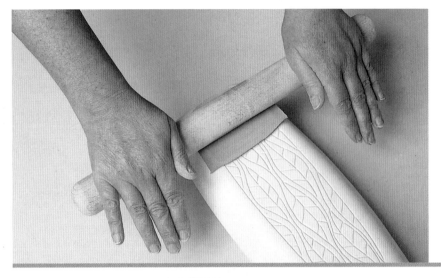

5 MAKING THE HANDLES Using some of the excess slab removed from the mould, cut out two sections of clay, which will fit over the ends of the relief pattern on the base of the dish.

Roll the sections of slab over the relief to ensure that the pattern is transferred to the clay in the same way as for the rim of the dish.

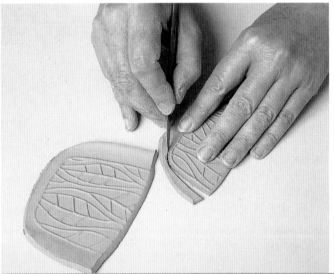

6 Lift the small slabs off the base of the mould and place them on the work surface. Very carefully cut around the pattern, leaving about 6 mm (¼ in.) around the outer edge of the relief. Run a finger around this edge when it is cut out to soften and round it off.

Cut the handle to a shape and size that suits your mould. Start by cutting a larger one because you can always cut it down further.

7 Mark the position of the handle on the side of the dish. Score and slip the area and the edge of the handle. Fix the handle in place and hold it in position for a second or two until the sections bond.

Roll a tiny coil of soft clay, and reinforce the join on the underside of the handle. Repeat the process for the other handle. Allow the dish to dry slowly to avoid the shape warping.

SEE ALSO
Basic skills: *Rolling slabs, pages 26–27* **Glaze recipes:** *pages 120–121*

MAKING TILES
AND A LOW RELIEF

There are several ways of making tiles. They can be cut from rolled out slabs of clay, using a template or a tile-cutter, or pressed into the mould, or slip cast in moulds.

MAKING TILES

It is important to dry your tiles slowly and evenly before firing to prevent the clay from warping. Some potters dry their tiles on wire racks so that air can circulate around them at all times, while others dry them between weighted boards. Using a grogged clay body will help reduce the tendency to warp.

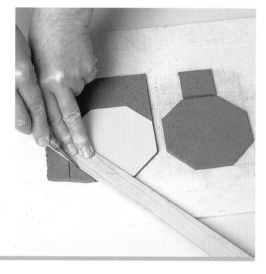

1 USING TEMPLATES The simplest method of making tiles is to roll a slab of clay as shown on pages 26–27, and then cut around paper or cardboard templates. Your tiles do not have to be square. However, if you make more complicated designs, it is important to measure and cut out templates accurately for a good fit.

Lower the wire as you cut each slab.

2 USING A HARP A clay harp allows you to cut evenly thick slabs of clay. When cutting a block of clay, you lower the wire to the next notch as each slab is cut. Although a harp is not essential, it is very useful if you intend to make a lot of tiles. The tiles will still need to be cut to shape.

3 USING A TILE CUTTER You will still have to roll or harp the slabs of clay, but the tiles will be identical in size when you use a tile cutter. It is a useful tool if you want to make a lot of tiles quickly.

CREATING A LOW RELIEF

Tiles are wonderful surfaces to decorate. However, they do not have to be flat. Sprigs will create quick and interesting low relief detail. Try the sprig moulds you made on page 94 to see how they look. Other examples of sprig decoration can be found in the Surface Decoration Library on pages 108–119.

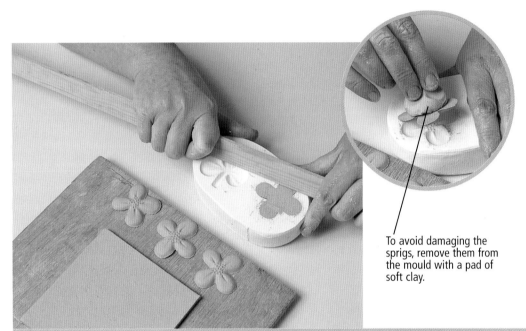

To avoid damaging the sprigs, remove them from the mould with a pad of soft clay.

1 **MAKING SPRIGS** Press a small amount of soft clay into the sprig mould, making sure it fills the space thoroughly. Remove the excess clay by dragging a roller guide over the surface. Make sure the guide is flat on the plaster mould and take care not to pull the clay out of the mould. You may need to practise a little.

To neaten around the edge of each sprig, remove excess slip with a wooden modelling tool or a damp paintbrush.

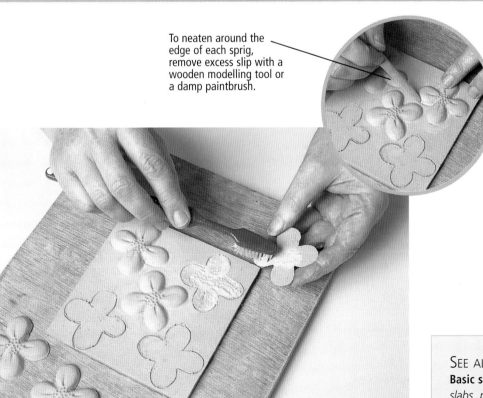

2 **THE DESIGN** Arrange the sprigs on the tile. Score around each one with a pointed tool to mark its position.

Score and slip the marked positions and the underside of each sprig. Fix the sprigs securely in place while squeezing out any air.

SEE ALSO
Basic skills: *Rolling slabs, pages 26–27*

Techniques: *Making a draped slab and sprig mould, pages 94–96*

SLIP-DECORATED TILE PANEL

This project incorporates several slip decoration techniques on a panel of tiles. Before you start, think about the design. This example is loosely based on a 1950s interior surface pattern, and is quite abstract. Whatever your design, it will be more successful if you do not make it too complicated, and if you start with only a small palette of colours.

After bisque firing to 1000°C (1832°F) the tiles were sponged with an earthenware transparent glaze and fired to 1080°C (1976°F) in an electric kiln.

YOU WILL NEED

MATERIALS
Clay: grogged red
   earthenware
Paper
Newspaper

FOR DECORATION
Slips
Sponge

TOOLS
Potter's pin

1 PREPARATION AND MASKING

Make nine tiles of your chosen size. Paint three coats of white slip on the tiles. Use the paper-resist method described on page 38 to mask out one corner of the panel with strips of newspaper to form a square about 13 mm (½ in.) bigger than the corner tile. Fill the square with paper leaf shapes in a random pattern.

The first coat of slip colour should be lightly sponged over the design.

Allow some base colour to show through.

TIPS FOR SUCCESS

- Work out your design to scale on paper. Think through the slip colour sequence, and make working notes.
- Cut out all your paper shapes in advance, and check that they work on your paper design.
- Make your tiles 10–15 cm (4–6 in.) square to begin with. This will make a 30.5–45.5 cm (12–18 in.) square panel before firing.

- Use an open-textured, natural sponge to build up interesting surface detail when applying slip.
- To avoid smearing the pattern, touch-dry each area of slip decoration with a hair-dryer before starting the next section.

Sponge a different colour slip inside the stencil.

To mask off the area covered with slip, cover with the negative (cutout) outline of the paper leaf.

2 Remove the resist strips around the corner square.

Mask out a rectangular area on the opposite side of the panel. Lay one long leaf shape within the rectangle. Sponge a slip colour over the top. Carefully remove the leaf from the centre using a potter's pin.

3 **BUILDING UP THE PATTERN** Continue to build up the design by masking off adjacent sections of the panel and filling them with paper shapes, or just blocks of colour.

Think about the balance of colour in your design, and build up the palette by sponging one colour lightly over another so that the first one, or even the base colour, still shows through. Work over the surface as if it were one canvas rather than nine sections.

To unseal the tiles before drying, cut around them with a sharp knife.

4 When all the blocks of colour have been completed, carefully remove the small paper shapes from each individual area with a potter's pin.

5 Draw sgraffito lines through the slip to reveal the colour of the clay beneath. For straight lines, use a ruler or draw freehand.

Build up the design with leaves, and draw into blank areas to fill the space.

SEE ALSO
Decorating: *Slip decoration, page 37; Sgraffito, page 39*

Glaze recipes: *pages 120–121*

COLOURED CLAYS

Different coloured clays can be mixed together to create an agate pattern. The combinations work best if you use clays with a similar shrinkage rate, but some potters use a range of clays to achieve the irregular shrinkage effect that is created when the work is fired. Here you will learn how to combine coloured clays to make agate and how to laminate clays together to form patterns for millefiore decoration.

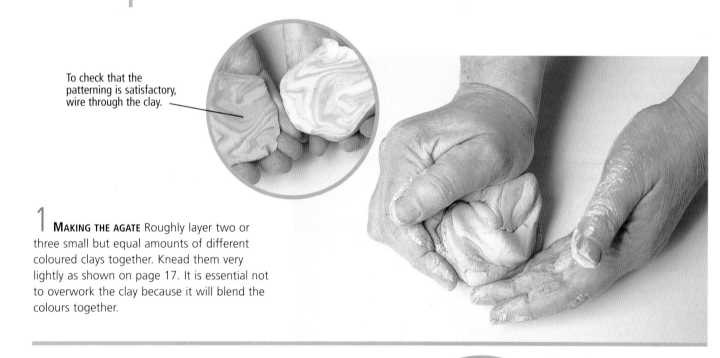

To check that the patterning is satisfactory, wire through the clay.

1 **MAKING THE AGATE** Roughly layer two or three small but equal amounts of different coloured clays together. Knead them very lightly as shown on page 17. It is essential not to overwork the clay because it will blend the colours together.

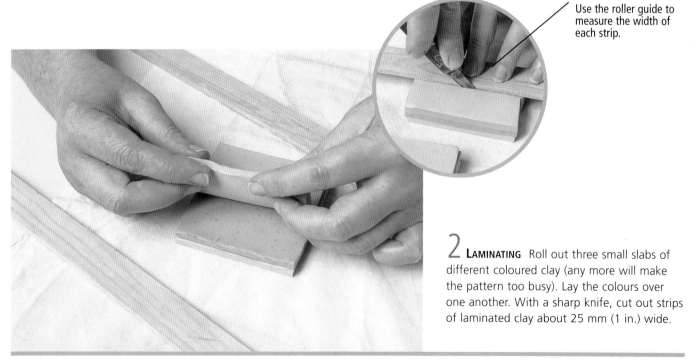

Use the roller guide to measure the width of each strip.

2 **LAMINATING** Roll out three small slabs of different coloured clay (any more will make the pattern too busy). Lay the colours over one another. With a sharp knife, cut out strips of laminated clay about 25 mm (1 in.) wide.

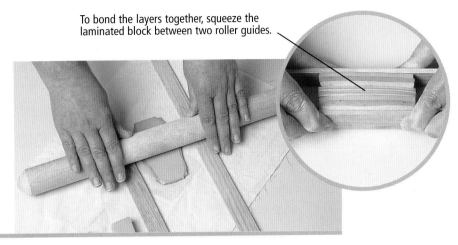

To bond the layers together, squeeze the laminated block between two roller guides.

3 **BUILDING UP PATTERNS** Re-roll one of the strips to the thickness of your roller guide. Cut another strip from this the same size as the original.

Sandwich the re-rolled strip between the two thicker strips. The thickness of the different colours should make an interesting combination.

4 **REASSEMBLING THE PATTERN** With a sharp knife, cut the laminated block of clay into thin strips. Cut the small strips into smaller pieces. Form different patterns with the pieces.

You may need a little slip or water to help reassemble small parts.

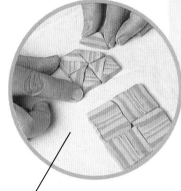

It is a good idea to reassemble the parts on a sheet of cotton.

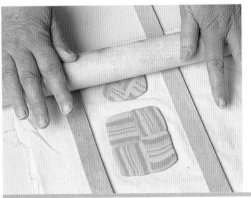

5 **RE-ROLLING** Roll the laminated patterns to the thickness of the roller guides.

6 These samples are quite small, but patterns can be built up in endless combinations to make slabbed forms or items of jewellery. To make more creative forms, tiny segments of laminated clay can be constructed inside moulds.

SEE ALSO
Getting started: Clay preparation, pages 16–17

Basic skills: Colouring clay, page 33

PROJECT 12 AGATE PORCELAIN BOX

This project is the most difficult in the book, mainly because porcelain behaves differently from other clays, but also because the slabs are much thinner than any we have worked with so far. Do not be disappointed if the project does not work the first time. You will find that an understanding of porcelain clay only comes with practice.

The box was bisque fired to 1000°C (1832°F) before being dipped in stoneware transparent glaze and fired to 1280°C (2336°F) with a half-hour soak at the top temperature.

YOU WILL NEED

MATERIALS

Clay: porcelain, coloured clays
Template parts:
2 x 8 cm (3 in.) squares.
1 x 10 cm (4 in.) square
4 x 8 x 12 cm (3 x 4¾ in.) sections
Extra piece for the locating rim of the lid
Cotton sheets

TOOLS

Roller guides
Scalpel
Biscuit cutter or cardboard template
Craft knife

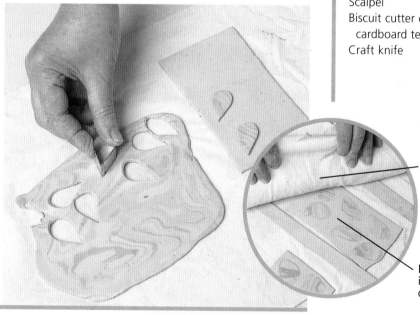

1 **MAKING THE BOX** Roll out a thin sheet of agate porcelain no thicker than 6 mm (¼ in.). Roll out a large, thin sheet of plain porcelain. Cut out all the parts to your box.

Using either a small biscuit cutter or a cardboard template, cut out shapes from the agate slab. Position them on all the box sections except the 10 cm (4 in.) square.

Reposition your r[...] guides either side [...] the sections. La[...] clean sheet of c[...] over the top.

Roll the agate into the surface of the porcelain.

TIPS FOR SUCCESS
- Roll out your slabs on clean sheets of cotton fabric.
- Roll coloured clays separately from the porcelain to avoid contamination.
- Make sure your work area is very clean.
- Clean your tools regularly; even tiny specks can spoil the surface of the porcelain.
- Cut out paper or card templates for all parts of the box before starting.
- Use porcelain slip to stick the agate shapes onto the slab sections.

2 Cut the sections back to shape using the templates. Add a little stamp detail to the design if you choose.

Mitre the four sides of the base square and three sides of each side panel, and then join them together as demonstrated on page 66.

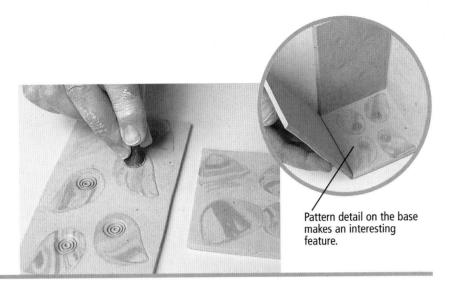

Pattern detail on the base makes an interesting feature.

3 **MAKING THE LID** Position the patterned section on the 10 cm (4 in.) square. Lightly mark the outline. Cut an 8 cm (3 in.) square within the marked outline. Score and slip the two sections. Fit them together so that the patterned square is raised from the larger section.

Score and slip the lid and rim surfaces.

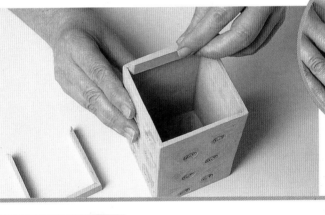

4 Cut four porcelain strips of about 1 x 8 cm (³⁄₈ x 3 in.) from your slab scraps. Measure each piece to fit inside the box. Mitre the ends of the strips. Join them together with a little slip to form the locating rim of the lid.

• Dry the lid in place to avoid distortion.

5 **ADDING DETAIL** Add carved detail to the box but handle it very carefully. Use the side of a craft knife blade to carve shallow detail along the length of each side, but do not overwork the surface. Remember, less is sometimes more.

Allow the box to dry out slowly and evenly before firing.

SEE ALSO
Decorating: *Stamps, page 34*
Glaze recipes: *pages 120–121*
Techniques: *Building with firm slabs, pages 66–67*

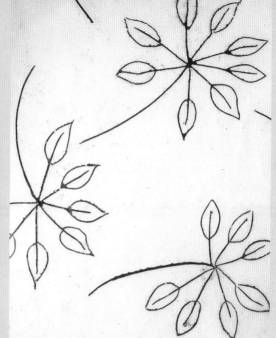

SURFACE DECORATION LIBRARY

On pages 110–119 you will find examples of all the surface decoration techniques demonstrated in Getting Started (see pages 34–47). All of the examples are within the capabilities of the beginner, and all are open to individual interpretation.

All the samples were fired in an electric kiln for both bisque and secondary treatment, except for those that are Raku and smoke fired (see pages 115 and 116).

On pages 120–121 you will find glaze recipes. If you explain your requirements, your supplier should be able to recommend glazes that are similar to the commercial examples shown.

Refer to the Glossary on pages 122–123 for definitions of terms you do not understand.

Earthenware slip decoration

Sponging
Clay type: Red earthenware clay.
Technique: Brushed, white slip base.
Yellow and blue slip applied lightly
with natural sponge. Transparent
glaze applied.
Firing: Fired to 1080°C (1976°F).

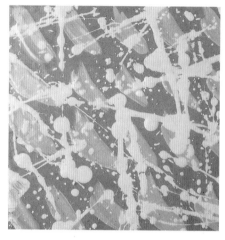

Brushing and spattering
Clay type: Red earthenware clay.
Technique: Brushed, blue slip base.
Yellow brush strokes applied when
touch dry. White slip spattered over
surface. Transparent glaze applied.
Firing: Fired to 1080°C (1976°F).

Marbling
Clay type: Red earthenware clay.
Technique: Dipped, white slip base.
Yellow and blue slip trailed to form
marbling. Transparent glaze applied.
Firing: Fired to 1080°C (1976°F).

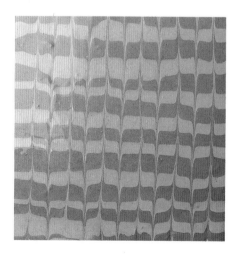

Feathering
Clay type: Red earthenware clay.
Technique: Blue slip base. Yellow
slip-trailed lines, feathered. Transparent
glaze applied.
Firing: Fired to 1080°C (1976°F).

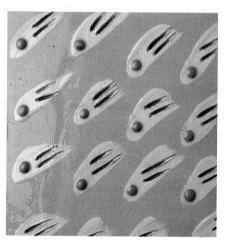

Combined techniques
Clay type: Red earthenware clay.
Technique: Brushed, blue slip base.
Yellow brush strokes; green slip-trailed
dots; sgraffito detail. Transparent
glaze applied.
Firing: Fired to 1080°C (1976°F).

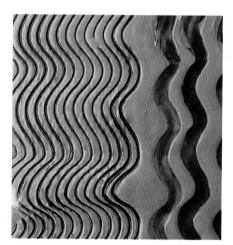

Combing
Clay type: Red earthenware clay.
Technique: Blue slip combed with a
toothed tool and fingers. Transparent
glaze applied.
Firing: Fired to 1080°C (1976°F).

SLIP TRAILING
Clay type: Red earthenware clay.
Technique: Blue slip trailed onto wet, yellow base so pattern merges into background. Transparent glaze applied.
Firing: Fired to 1080°C (1976°F).

SLIP TRAILING
Clay type: Red earthenware clay, leather hard.
Technique: Yellow slip trailed to form a raised pattern. Transparent glaze applied.
Firing: Fired to 1080°C (1976°F).

SGRAFFITO
Clay type: Red earthenware clay.
Technique: Brushed, white slip base; simple sgraffito pattern. Honey glaze applied.
Firing: Fired to 1080°C (1976°F).

LACE AND SLIP
Clay type: Red earthenware clay.
Technique: Lace fabric rolled into clay; painted white slip over fabric. Honey glaze applied.
Firing: Fired to 1080°C (1976°F).

STENCIL PAPER RESIST
Clay type: Red earthenware clay.
Technique: Blue, yellow and red stencilled slip design. Burnished; coated with wax polish.
Firing: Bisque fired to 1000°C (1832°F).

PAPER RESIST
Clay type: Red earthenware clay.
Technique: Brushed, white slip base. Paper-resist pattern sponged over lightly with green and black slip. Transparent glaze applied.
Firing: Fired to 1080°C (1976°F).

INLAY

Clay type: Red earthenware clay.
Technique: White slip inlaid design.
Honey glaze applied.
Firing: Fired to 1080°C (1976°F).

WAX AND SLIP

Clay type: Red earthenware clay.
Technique: White slip base, wax
pattern. Green slip painted over top.
Transparent glaze applied.
Firing: Fired to 1080°C (1976°F).

INLAY

Clay type: White earthenware clay.
Technique: Green slip inlaid design.
Transparent glaze applied.
Firing: Fired to 1080°C (1976°F).

SGRAFFITO REPEAT

Clay type: Red earthenware.
Technique: White slip base; green and
yellow lightly sponged over top. Repeat
sgraffito pattern applied.
Firing: Fired to 1080°C (1976°F).

Earthenware glaze techniques

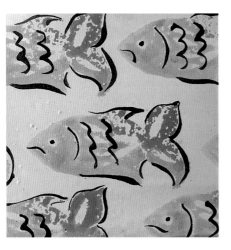

Majolica technique
Clay type: Red earthenware clay.
Technique: White tin glaze base.
Underglaze colours applied with precut
sponges. Black outline applied with a
fine brush.
Firing: Fired to 1100°C (2012°F) with a
15-minute soak.

Majolica technique
Clay type: Red earthenware clay.
Technique: White tin glaze base.
Underglaze colours applied with a
selection of precut sponges.
Firing: Fired to 1100°C (2012°F) with a
15-minute soak.

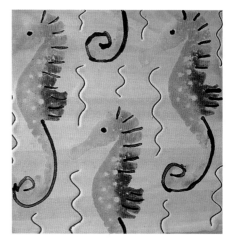

Majolica technique
Clay type: Red earthenware clay.
Technique: White tin glaze base. Thin
wash of underglaze colour. Seahorses
applied with precut sponges and
outlined by brush. Waves scratched
through glaze with sharp tool.
Firing: Fired to 1100°C (2012°F) with a
15-minute soak.

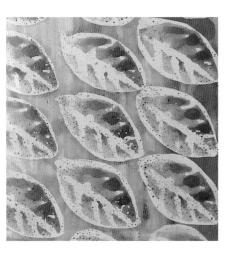

Majolica technique
Clay type: Red earthenware clay.
Technique: White tin glaze base.
Pattern applied with precut sponges and
underglaze colours, painted over with
wax. Final wash colour over surface
applied with soft brush.
Firing: Fired to 1100°C (2012°F) with a
15-minute soak.

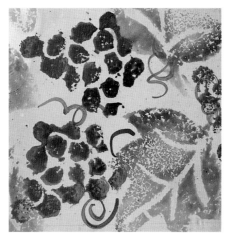

Majolica technique
Variation on the previous designs.

Majolica variation
Clay type: Red earthenware clay.
Technique: White tin glaze base. Wax
pattern. Cobalt carbonate wash.
Firing: Fired to 1100°C (2012°F) with a
15-minute soak at the top temperature.

CARVING THROUGH GLAZE
Clay type: Red earthenware clay.
Technique: White tin glaze base. Pattern scraped through to clay with sharp tool.
Firing: Fired to 1100°C (2012°F) with a 15-minute soak.

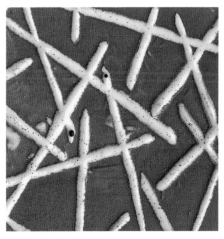

WIPING AWAY
Clay type: Textured red earthenware.
Technique: Tin glaze applied and wiped back so glaze in texture only.
Firing: Fired to 1100°C (2012°F) with a 15-minute soak.

SIMPLE WAX RESIST
Clay type: Red earthenware clay.
Technique: Wax-resist pattern on bisque-fired clay. White tin glaze.
Firing: Fired to 1100°C (2012°F) with a 15-minute soak.

OXIDE AND GLAZE
Clay type: Red earthenware clay.
Technique: Wax-resist pattern on fired clay. Manganese dioxide wash. Wax resist. Lightly sponged coat white tin glaze.
Firing: Fired to 1100°C (2012°F) with a 15-minute soak.

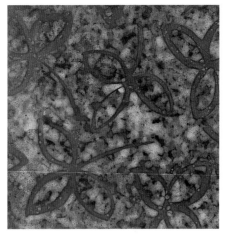

MULTIPLE GLAZE
Clay type: Red earthenware clay.
Technique: Dipped, blue glaze base. Wax-resist pattern. White tin glaze sponged lightly over top. Orange glaze sponged in selected areas.
Firing: Fired to 1080°C (1976°F).

CARVED SURFACE
Clay type: Red earthenware clay.
Technique: Leather hard clay. Carved pattern. Transparent glaze applied.
Firing: Fired to 1080°C (1976°F).

Low fire techniques

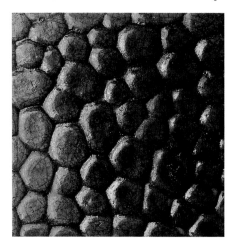

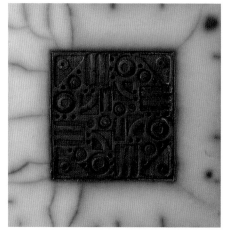

Raku glaze
Clay type: Grogged Raku clay.
Technique: Turquoise glaze with light reduction in sawdust for lustre effect.
Firing: Fired to approximately 900°C (1652°F) in a Raku kiln.

Raku resist
Clay type: White, grogged stoneware clay.
Technique: Partly textured and burnished. Raku resist slip and glaze, both removed after firing. Wax polish.
Firing: Fired in Raku kiln until glaze melts. Light smoking in sawdust for crazed surface effect.

Smoke firing
Clay type: White, grogged stoneware clay.
Technique: Carved low relief.
Firing: Fired over several hours in sawdust-filled bin with seaweed and sprinkling of copper carbonate and rock salt for pink effects.

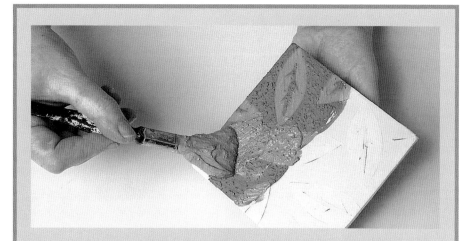

Preparing resist surface for smoke firing
To prepare a surface for smoke firing, apply a masking-tape pattern of your choice to a bisque-fired, burnished surface. Paint over the pattern with a fairly thick layer of grogged clay slurry. Allow the slurry to dry thoroughly before smoke firing (see page 20).

Resist smoke fired
Technique: Masking-tape pattern burns and carbon is absorbed into surface. Resist slurry prevents smoke being absorbed where not required.
Firing: Fired in sawdust or newspaper.

BRUSH-ON GLAZE

Clay type: White earthenware clay.
Technique: Commercial, turquoise glaze applied by brush in several coats over textured surface.
Firing: Fired to 1000°C (1832°F). If for functional ware, check with supplier that glaze is suitable.

MULTIPLE BRUSH-ON GLAZE

Three different brush-on glazes provide a variation on the previous example fired to 1000°C (1832°F).

STONEWARE GLAZE TECHNIQUES

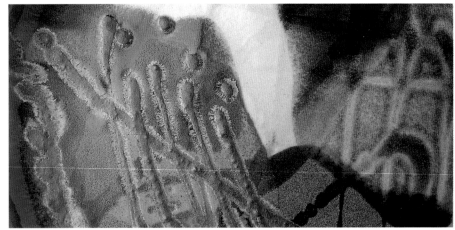

BRUSH-ON GLAZE

Clay type: Buff stoneware clay.
Technique: Part-textured surface. Commercial brush-on stoneware glaze designed to break over textured surfaces.
Firing: Fired to 1260°C (2300°F) with a 30-minute soak.

POURING METHOD

Clay type: White stoneware.
Technique: Multiple glazes, some poured over surface, others slip trailed for special effects.
Firing: Fired to 1280°C (2336°F) with a 30-minute soak.

Latex resist
Clay type: White stoneware clay.
Technique: Latex pattern applied through fine-nozzle slip trailer. Glaze poured over surface. Latex removed when glaze dried.
Firing: Fired to 1280°C (2336°F) with a 30-minute soak.

Wax resist with multiple glaze
Clay type: White stoneware clay.
Technique: Dipped dolomite-glaze base. Wax-resist pattern. Black and red glazes sponged over surface.
Firing: Fired to 1280°C (2336°F) with a 30-minute soak.

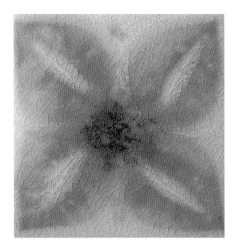

Sponge patterns
Clay type: White stoneware clay.
Technique: Dipped dolomite-glaze base. Orange-red glaze applied with precut sponges. Black glaze applied in centre.
Firing: Fired to 1260°C (2300°F) with a 30-minute soak.

Oxide on glaze
Clay type: White stoneware clay.
Technique: Dipped, white, stoneware, tin glaze base. Painted cobalt-oxide decoration.
Firing: Fired to 2336°F (1280°C) with a 30-minute soak.

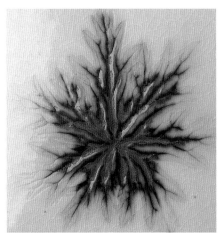

Oxide in texture
Clay type: Porcelain clay.
Technique: Copper oxide rubbed into leaf texture. Transparent glaze applied.
Firing: Fired to 1280°C (2336°F) with a 30-minute soak.

Oxide with wiped-back glaze
Clay type: Buff stoneware clay.
Technique: Thick copper-oxide wash over texture. Dipped in transparent glaze, wiped back over texture.
Firing: Fired to 1260°C (2300°F) with a 30-minute soak.

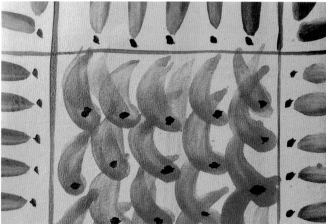

REACTIVE GLAZE
Clay type: Buff stoneware clay.
Technique: Commercial brush-on glaze applied over textured surface. Commercial reactive glaze sponged over top to change colour.
Firing: Fired to 1260°C (2300°F) with a 15-minute soak.

UNDERGLAZE DECORATION
Clay type: White stoneware clay.
Technique: Underglaze colours applied with brushes to form pattern. Covered with transparent glaze.
Firing: Fired to 1260°C (2300°F) with a 15-minute soak.

SPRIG LOW RELIEF

SPRIGS FROM NATURAL FORMS
Clay type: White stoneware clay.
Technique: Sprigs made from beach finds. Blue glaze applied, wiped back over sprigs.
Firing: Fired to 1245°C (2273°F) with a 20-minute soak.

SPRIGS, OXIDE AND GLAZE
Clay type: Buff stoneware clay.
Technique: Manganese-dioxide wash over sprigs. Dry-ash glaze sponged over surface.
Firing: Fired to 1260°C (2300°F) with a 15-minute soak.

SINGLE SPRIG WITH REACTIVE SLIP AND GLAZE
Clay type: Buff stoneware clay.
Technique: Commercial reactive slip, covered with commercial grey or white reactive glaze (designed to be used together).
Firing: Fired to 1260°C (2300°F) with a 30-minute soak.

UNUSUAL FINISHES

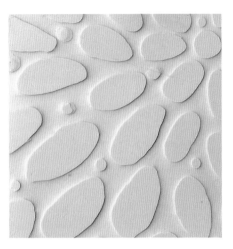

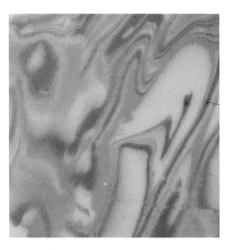

PIERCING
Clay type: White stoneware clay.
Technique: Pierced or cut-out pattern.
Simple black glaze.
Firing: Fired to 1260°C (2300°F) with a
30-minute soak.

SHELLAC RESIST
Clay type: Porcelain clay.
Technique: Shellac resist. Clay wiped
away around resist.
Firing: Fired to 1280°C (2336°F);
unglazed.

AGATE
Clay type: Coloured porcelain clays.
Technique: Transparent glaze applied.
Firing: Fired to 1280°C (2336°F) with a
30-minute soak.

ENAMELS AND LUSTRE

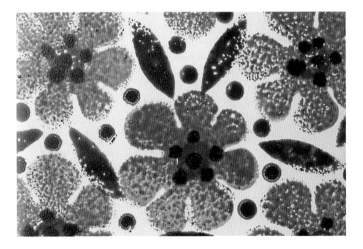

ON-GLAZE ENAMEL
Clay type: Commercial white, glazed
tile.
Technique: Enamel colours applied with
precut sponges.
Firing: Fired very slowly to 730°C
(1341°F) to allow oil medium to
burn off.

LUSTRE
Clay type: Porcelain clay.
Technique: Textured pattern with
sections of transparent glaze. Selection
of lustre colours applied to glazed and
unglazed areas.
Firing: Fired slowly to 730°C (1341°F).

GLAZE RECIPES

These glaze recipes represent those used in the projects in this book. If you prefer not to mix your glazes from the raw ingredients, your pottery supplier will be able to advise you on suitable pre-prepared alternatives.

TRANSPARENT EARTHENWARE LEAD GLAZE

	Parts dry weight
Lead bi-silicate	65
Whiting	10
Potash feldspar	15
China clay	10

Fire to 1080°C (1976°F).

This is a versatile, transparent glaze that can be coloured by oxides or stains for variation. If intended for use on domestic ware, test for safety regarding the release of metals. Testing can be arranged through your pottery supplier. If you have safety concerns, borax frit can be used instead of lead.

Add 3 per cent red iron oxide and 0.5 per cent manganese dioxide to make orange; 5 per cent cobalt oxide to give a good blue; and 3 per cent copper oxide to give deep green.

This glaze was used for several samples in the Surface Decoration Library (see pages 108–119) in both transparent and coloured forms on Project 1 (see pages 52–53) and Project 8 (see pages 84–87).

EARTHENWARE TIN GLAZE

	Parts dry weight
Lead bi-silicate	26
Borax frit	7
Ball clay	6
China clay	4
Tin oxide	3
Bentonite	1

Fire to 1080–1120°C (1980–2050°F)

This is a good stable white tin glaze that is ideal for red clay and majolica decoration. It breaks nicely over texture to reveal a rich red colour.

This glaze was used to decorate Project 7 (see pages 80–81), and several samples in the Surface Decoration Library (see pages 108–119) .

TRANSPARENT STONEWARE

	Parts dry weight
Cornish stone	85
Whiting	15
Plus 2 per cent Bentonite	

Fire to 1260–1280°C (2300–2336°F) with a 30-minute soak.

Add 4 per cent tin oxide to make white; 4 per cent glaze stain generally makes a good colour but you will need to experiment for best results.

This glaze was used in transparent and coloured form for several samples in the Surface Decoration Library (see pages 108–119), Project 6 (see pages 72–73), Project 10 (see pages 97–99) and Project 12 (see pages 106–107).

DOLOMITE STONEWARE

	Parts dry weight
Potash feldspar	30
Dolomite	20
Whiting	15
China clay	20
Flint	5

Fire to 1265°C (2309°F).

This glaze was used over an oxide wash for Project 3 (see pages 60–61) and in combination with other glazes for samples in the Surface Decoration Library (see pages 108–119).

RAKU GLAZES

TURQUOISE LUSTRE GLAZE

	Parts dry weight
High alkaline frit	50
Borax frit	20
Copper oxide	4
Bentonite	3

Fire to 1000°C (1832°F).

This glaze produces a good turquoise when applied thickly and copper-red lustre when heavily reduced in sawdust. It was used to decorate Project 9 (see pages 90–93) and a sample in the Surface Decoration Library (see page 115).

RAKU RESIST GLAZE

	Parts dry weight
High alkali frit	46
Borax frit	46
China clay	8

For this method of firing, the glaze needs only to barely melt. It should be applied over the resist slip by pouring or brushing carefully. When fired, the glaze shells off.

It was used to decorate Project 5 (see pages 68–69).

All other glazes used in the book are commercial. There is a vast selection of ready-made glazes available; ask your supplier for information.

RAKU RESIST SLIP

3 parts China clay
2 parts flint

Use a cup to measure the ingredients and mix them with water to the consistency of cream. The slip can be applied to the surface by pouring or brushing, but needs to be at least 3 mm (¹⁄₈ in.) thick. It is applied to the bisque-fired pot before glazing.

This dish has been sponged with several coats of a stoneware glaze to give a beautiful finish.

Glossary of terms

ALUMINA One of the three main components of glaze, it has a very high melting point. Usually added to a glaze in the form of powdered clay. Hydrated alumina is used as a constituent of kiln wash.

BALL CLAY Fine plastic clay, usually white or off-white after firing. So named because the clay is transported in round lumps.

BANDING WHEEL A turntable operated by hand and used for building and decorating.

BAT Plaster or wooden disk for throwing or moving pots without handling them, or for drying clay.

BAT WASH Mixture of alumina and China clay used as a protective coating for kiln shelves.

BEATING See paddling.

BISQUE (biscuit) Clay ware after the first firing, usually around 1000°C (1832°F).

BISQUE FIRING The first firing of pottery to mature the clay and make it permanent. Pots may be stacked inside or on top of one another because there is no glaze to make them stick together.

BODY The term used to describe a particular mixture of clay, such as earthenware body.

BURNISHING Process of polishing leather-hard clay with smooth pebbles or spoons to achieve a shiny surface. Used to compact the clay and as a decorative feature.

CALCINATION Method of purifying by heating a compound or oxide to drive out carbon gases or water. Also reduces plasticity in powdered clays.

CASTING Making pots by pouring liquid clay into a plaster mould.

CASTING SLIP Liquid slip used when making objects in plaster moulds.

CERAMIC Clay form that is fired in a kiln.

CHINA CLAY Pure-white-burning, nonplastic body clay, usually used in combination with other clays or in glazes.

COILING Forming a pot from coils or ropes of clay. Variations include flattened coils.

COLLARING Action of squeezing around a pot to draw the shape inwards, especially used in throwing.

COMBING Method of decoration using fingers or a toothed tool to scrape a series of lines through slip.

COTTLE Wall used to surround a shape to be cast in plaster.

CRAZING Fine cracks caused by contraction of glaze over the clay surface.

DIPPING Applying a slip or glaze by immersion.

EARTHENWARE Pottery fired at a relatively low temperature. The body remains porous and usually requires glazing if it is to be used for domestic ware.

ELEMENT Metal heating coil in an electric kiln.

ENAMEL Low-firing, commercially manufactured colour that is painted onto a fired surface and refired to melt it into the glaze.

FEATHERING Decoration made by drawing a sharp tip through wet slip.

FIRING Process by which clay ware is heated in a kiln to harden or glaze it.

FIRING CHAMBER Interior of a kiln in which pottery is fired.

FIRING CYCLE Gradual raising and lowering of the temperature of a kiln to fire pottery.

FLANGE Rim on the inside of a lid and the ledge around the inside of a pot's opening used to locate the lid and hold it securely in place. Sometimes called a gallery.

FOOT Base on which a piece of pottery rests.

FOOT RING Circle of clay that forms the base of a pot, allowing it to stand evenly.

GALLERY See flange.

GLAZE Thin, glassy layer on the surface of pottery.

GLAZE STAIN Commercially manufactured colourant that is added to glaze.

GREENWARE Unfired clay ware.

GROG Fired clay that is ground into particles, ranging from a fine dust to coarse sand. When added to soft clay, it adds strength, resists warping and helps reduce thermal shock.

HAND BUILDING Making pottery without the use of a potter's wheel, either by coiling, pinching or slabbing.

INCISE Process of carving or cutting a design into a raw clay surface.

KIDNEY Metal, plastic, wood or rubber scraper.

KILN Device in which pottery is fired.

KILN SUPPORTS Refractory pieces used to separate and support kiln shelves and pottery during firing.

KNEADING Method of dispersing moisture uniformly through clay and removing air to prepare the clay for use.

LATEX Rubber-based glue that can be used as a peelable resist when decorating pottery.

LEATHER HARD Clay that is stiff and damp but no longer plastic. It is hard enough to be handled without distorting, but can still be joined.

LUSTRE Metallic salts added in a thin layer over glaze to produce a lustrous metallic finish.

MAJOLICA (MAIOLICA) Name given to tin glaze earthenware with in-glaze decoration.

MOULD Plaster form used with soft clay.

ON-GLAZE COLOUR See enamel.

PADDLING Tapping a wooden tool against a piece of clay to refine the shape.

PLASTIC CLAY Clay that can be manipulated without losing its shape.

PORCELAIN Fine, high-firing white clay that becomes translucent when fired.

POTTER'S PLASTER Used for making absorbent moulds. The plaster hardens through chemical reaction with water. Also called plaster of paris.

PRESS MOULDING Pressing slabs of clay into or over moulds to form shapes.

PROP Tube of refractory clay used for supporting kiln shelves during firing.

PYROMETER Equipment for measuring the temperature in a kiln during firing.

RAKU A firing technique in which pots are placed directly into a hot kiln and removed when red-hot.

REFRACTORY Ceramic materials that are resistant to high temperatures.

RESIST Decorative medium such as wax, latex or paper used to prevent slip or glaze from sticking to the surface of pottery.

RIB Wooden or plastic tool used to lift the walls of thrown pots.

SCRAPER Thin metal and plastic tool used to refine clay surfaces. It can be straight or kidney-shaped.

SGRAFFITO Scratching through a layer of clay, slip or glaze to reveal the colour underneath.

SHORT Term used to describe soft clay lacking plasticity, which cracks when bent.

SLABBING Making pottery from slabs of clay.

SLIP Liquid clay.

SLIP TRAILING Decorating with coloured slip squeezed through a nozzle.

SOAK Allowing the kiln to remain at a specific temperature for a length of time to smooth and settle a glaze.

SOFT SOAP Semi-liquid soap used to form a release in mouldmaking.

SPONGING Decorative method of applying slip or glaze, or of cleaning the surface of pottery before firing.

SPRIG Moulded clay form used as an applied decoration.

STAIN Unfired colour used for decorating pottery, or a ceramic pigment used to add colour to glazes and bodies.

STILT Small stand used to support pots during firing to prevent glazed surfaces coming into contact with the kiln shelf.

STONEWARE Vitrified clay, usually fired above 1200°C (2192°F).

TERRACOTTA Iron-bearing earthenware clay that matures at low temperatures and fires to a rich, red colour.

THERMAL SHOCK Sudden increase or decrease in temperature that puts great stress on a fired clay body, causing it to crack.

TOXIC Any ceramic material – solid, gaseous or liquid – that is injurious to health.

TURNING Removing spare clay from the base of a thrown pot with a sharp loop tool while the pot revolves on the wheel.

UNDERGLAZE Colour that is usually applied to greenware or bisque-fired pottery and, in most cases, covered with a glaze.

VITRIFICATION POINT Point at which clay particles fuse together.

VITRIFIED Refers to clays that have been fired at high temperatures, fusing the particles together so they become glasslike.

WAX RESIST Process of decorating by painting wax on a surface to resist a water-based covering.

WEDGING Method of preparing clay for use, or mixing different clays together to an even, air-free consistency.

ALEC TIRANTI LTD

70 High Street, Theale
Reading
Berkshire
RG7 5AR
Tel: +44 (0)118 930 2775
Email: enquiries@tiranti.co.uk
London shop: 27 Warren Street, London, W1T 5NB
Tel: +44 (0)207 636 8565
www.tiranti.co.uk

BATH POTTERS' SUPPLIES

Unit 18, Fourth Avenue
Westfield Trading Estate
Radstock, nr Bath
BA3 4XE
Tel: +44 (0)1761 411 077
www.bathpotters.co.uk

BRIAR WHEELS AND SUPPLIES LTD

Whitsbury Road
Fordingbridge
Hampshire
SP6 1NQ
Tel: +44 (0)1425 652 991
www.briarwheels.co.uk

COMMERICAL CLAY LTD

Sandbach Road
Corbrige
Stoke-on-Trent
Staffordshire
ST6 2DR
Tel: +44 (0)1782 274 448

CRAFTS COUNCIL UK

44a Pentonville Road
Islington
London
N1 9BY
Tel: +44 (0)207 278 7700
www.craftscouncil.org.uk

CRAFT POTTERS' ASSOCIATION OF GREAT BRITAIN

25 Foubert's Place
London
W1F 7QF
Tel: +44 (0)207 437 6781

Northern Kilns
Pilling Pottery
School Lane
Pilling
Lancashire
PR3 6HB
Tel: +44 (0)1253 790 307
www.northernkilns.com

Potclays Ltd
Brickkiln Lane
Stoke-on-Trent
ST4 4BP
Tel: +44 (0)1782 219 816
e-mail: sakes@potclays.co.uk
www.potclays.co.u

Pottery Crafts Ltd
Campbell Road
Stoke-on-Trent
Staffordshire
ST4 4ET
Tel: +44 (0)1782 745 000
www.potterycrafts.co.uk

Potter's Mate
Cust Hall
Tordes Field
Halstead
Essex
Tel: +44 (0)1787 237 704

Stow Potters' Wheels
4 Brocregin
Llangrannog
Llandysul
SA44 6AG
Tel: +44 (0)1239 654 300
Email: stowwheels@aol.com

Valentine Clays
The Sliphouse
18–20 Chell Street
Hanley
Stoke-on-Trent
ST1 6BA
Tel: +44 (0)1239 654 300
Email: stowwheels@aol.com

Examples of finished projects
ready to be fired.

INDEX

CREDITS

AUTHOR'S ACKNOWLEDGEMENTS

I would like to thank my husband, John, and children Nicola, Adam and Charlie for their patience and support while writing this book and Ian Howes, the photographer, for his kindness and humour.

Many thanks also to Jill Hampson for work on the decorative library and technical information; Jacqui Kruzewski and Mary and Simon Chappelhowe for the throwing techniques and projects and use of their studio for the photography of that section of the book.

With thanks to Peter Stokes of Commercial Clay Ltd for supplying the clay used in this book. Thanks also to PotClays Ltd and Pottery Crafts Ltd for supplying other materials used in this book.

I would like to dedicate this book to the memory of my dear friend Angela who was a prolific collector of my work and my greatest fan.

Quarto would like to thank the following manufacturers for allowing photographs to be reproduced in this book:
p18 Potclays and p12 Stow Potters Wheels